Pocket Cruising and Micro Adventures

A simple sailing life on a budget

A tribute to the joy of sailing and to the greatest experiences in the smallest crafts. The philosophy is equally simple: The joy of sailing is inversely proportional to the size of the boat.

Martin Anker Wiedemann

Pocket Cruising
and Micro Adventures

A simple sailing life on a budget

Previously published books by the author

With a Circle in Mind (2015)

Pocket Cruising og Mikroeventyr (2019) in Danish

Editor: Martin Anker Wiedemann
Proofreading and feedback: John Machell, Uwe Gräfer, Jens Wellejus, Oscar and Emil Wiedemann, and finally Mette Wiedemann

Publisher: BoD – Books on Demand, Copenhagen, Denmark

Print: BoD – Books on Demand, Norderstedt, Germany

ISBN: 978-87-4302-927-4

CONTENT

PREFACE

Dear sailor,

The purpose of this book is to display, what possibilities lie in front of you for becoming a cruising yachtsman on a modest budget with special emphasis on the wealth of small cruising yachts from the 1960's and 70's populating the marinas of Denmark and Northern Germany or commonly seen in the UK.

I wish to inspire you and offer you valuable things to reflect on, when choosing how to sail or what path to the sea will fit you, making your first experiences as sailor, skipper and boat owner.

Minimalism is the founding philosophy of the recommendations of this book, which expressly translates into just how little boat you will need to fulfill a meaningful sailing life? But it is by no means meant as a dogma. Each and every one of us should find exactly the sense and level fitting our needs and temperament. So if you simply cannot live without an ice cube machine onboard your tiny boat, you are still entitled to call yourself a minimalist in my perception.

The purpose of sailing an ever so little boat is to feel free. Free as a human being and free of worry, anxiety, hustle and bustle. Free to experience the joy of being in nature by sailing and by being part of the companionship, being in the same boat will give you.

In the first chapters of this book, a series of recommendations of strategies for fitting out and using a boat are offered. Including navigation, choice of engine, equipment, cooking, heating and water supply etc. This book is not thought of as a textbook on sailing, but as the sort of personal advice you would find at your local marina from experienced sailors. If you are new to sailing, you should therefore read one of the many proper textbooks on practical sailing, attend a sailing school and learn to navigate. But if you will benefit from some of my advice, my mission is completed.

The "pocket cruiser" is a modern concept, indicating that we speak about the smallest of boats. In America pocket cruisers are referred to as sailboats below 30-33 feet, which can seem just as meaningless as our self acclaimed standard of 26 feet (under the statute of the facebook group "Dansk Pocket Yacht Club"), when you consider that these boats of the 60's and 70's were thought of as regular family yachts and measured up to the 1/2 ton IOR offshore racing yardstick.

Just the same, the standard for a sensible first sailboat for a young family of today is negotiable or subject to a deliberate minimalistic choice for others.

My definition of a genuine pocket cruiser is a sailboat, you can cruise in and stay overnight. It is a boat you can sail and master on your own, get to your port of call - in both good or bad weather. The pocket cruiser should not be a statement nor a demonstrative deselection or denunciation of other ways of sailing but an expression of an active positive choice.

Hence, the selection of pocket cruisers on display in this book fall into two categories: The diminutive sailboats up untill 22 feet and the smaller family yachts between 23 and 26 feet. There is an enormeous selection of attractive second hand yachts in the upper end and almost the same amount of the most tiny ones.

I have limited myself to a selection of boats generally available in Denmark. You will however look in vane for some boat types. It has to be that way.

Finally, towards the end of this book, I will share my personal pocket cruising experience and how I found my way to sea.

Simple living: Putting the kettle on in the cockpit on a simple camping stove at anchor.

And just to put the finger on it: This is how not to do it. Safety at sea should not be taken as lightly, as I did in this picture from 2001.

My wife constantly feeds us
with hot coffee and
chocolate when underway.

1. WHY DO WE SAIL?

The essence of sailing

Why do we sail? That is the fundamental question. What parts of the essence of sailing do we pursue and cultivate? The simple answer is found in the latin proverb

"Navigare necesse est"

Sailing is necessary. A different answer might be: Because I can.

A common denominator for many small boat yachtsmen could be the freedom experienced in sailing, or it could be a variety of things we profit from sailing defining our individual approach at the essense of sailing. There are many aspects of sailing and individually we may see sailing as experiences in the framework of nature, as a personal development laboratory or something entirely different. Unlike any other leisure activity I can think of, owning and sailing a boat requires so many different competencies of us and there will always remain unexplored areas of competency to pursue.

Nature's room

Sailing is a mavellous opportunity to explore nature and the coasts, colours, scents and wildlife in the sea and along the coast. An opportunity to feel the earth moving physically and sensously. The everchanging nature in all its beauty and uncompromising toughness. The water, the light, the wind, the clouds and temperature. From relaxing bathing holiday to sheer survival and back again in no time at all.

The development laboratory

Training to dare daring. Making decisions and living with their consequences, getting acquainted with your personal physical and mental potential for better or worse. I dare a lot more today, than when I first headed to sea in a small keelboat many years ago. I have become a "brave chicken," in the sense that I retain the realism of fear when choosing my challenges.

"Nec temere. Nec timide!"

(Neither reckless nor timid - the motto of the Royal Danish Naval Academy, originally a quotation of admiral Niels Juel - 1629-1697)

The meditation room

Sailing is an activity of great meditative quality, which you can enjoy in your spare time. The challenge of the monotony of sailing is an aim in itself for emptying your mind, think of nothing and just being. The rythmic patterns of the boat - much resembling music - is a fantastic catalyst to transcend to a meditative state just like long stretches, where conversations dry out and stillness take their place. When sailing alone, I love to stand at the helm with the tiller in my back and eyes closed, becoming one with the boat and its movement, while my footing becomes grounded and solid.

The play room

Fun playing trips with like minded grown up girls and boys, ready for some rough fun in fresh conditions. Up with the spinnaker, trimming, experimenting. Racing could be exactly that kind of playground, where we unfold and have great fun.

The navigation room

Navigation is both an intellectual challenge and almost an artform of existential and spiritual proportions. I like to perform it with a gps as well as manually with a paper chart, hand bearing compass and ruler, noting the escapades in the log for reading later so I can relive the cruises.

It is the room between navigation and seamanship. Knowing the strengths and limitations of your boat with the crew. Where things are taken into consideration and a route best making use of wind, weather, landscape and sea is planned.

The coffee room

Pottering about in your homely bay or estuary. Brewing coffee and telling yarns. Here the social capital is growing and with interest. Weekend trips with culinary peaks and fitting rations of redwine in the officers' mess. Even in the colder outer season, talking into the night. Sailing as a way of spending time together.

Team expeditions

Sailing can be a shared experience with a hand picked crew, where the journey is an expedition in its own right and the goal just a waypoint to round; knowing that we are homeward bound again. The best thing about long passages is when we tune into the rythm of the ship, which is the spirit a good crew creates and is the social and maritime frame of the journey.

Life onboard

I just love the life onboard after provisioning, bunkering and stowing away personal gear, books and charts down below and making it work as an independent selfsustainable unit for days at sea without permanent power supply or fresh provisioning. Whether alone or with a friend or the family, I enjoy making my little ship work satisfactory under all conditions. Adjusting to the rythm of the ship and tuning into its movements in the swell.

Life in port

Lying in a cosy holiday port with new neighbours each and every other day. Driving your inner rythm down in a different gear than back home on dry land. Or literally going down to your home port and checking the mooring lines, fingering the sea charts or have a cup of coffee - or just sit and do nothing while staring in front of you. Clearing up and cleaning up to make a tight ship.

A successful cruise equals a happy crew. Especially in the early years, my wife Mette enjoyed port life as a reward for enduring the sailing. Now we both enjoy sailing as well as cosy time spent in port.

Fundamentally I love sailing as a happy dance, an elusive harmony, when everything falls into a higher unity, and the sheer joy and happiness enjoyed on your own or with a crew.

You need to figure out, which rooms fit your sailing perception or your sailing existence the best; Whatever floats your boat!

2. THE MICRO ADVENTURE

"If the whole is ever to gladden thee,
Then that whole in the smallest thing thou must see."
- Johann Wolfgang von Goethe

When it comes to pocket cruising, the idea of minimalism fits the concept of micro adventures like a hand in a glove.

Under way you have an enormeous amount of time for yourself. Your best friends are the binoculars. Everything out there in the horizon is interesting, when we have exhausted our energy and attention on sail trim and navigation.

My wife and I crossed the bay of Køge in the Øresund between Zealand and the Swedish coast in stinging heat and bothered by millions of annoying flies. "I want to see a seal" she suddenly burst out. "You cannot simply demand to see a seal," I replied. "Why of course I can. See!," she answered. I was already armed with the binoculars to keep a lookout for bouys and lights, so now I just had to add seals to my list! And half an hour later to my astonishment something dark was lying bopping on the surface a few hundred metres to port: A seal! Mette's self confidence soared after this experience. Thus, we created content, joy and experience for each other on a day, which was easy to hate because of a long tedious passage under engine, flies buzzing everywhere and a relentless stinging sun.

The adventure begins just outside of the breakwater. We don't have to circumnavigate the world. Micro adventures are created for us, who stay at home. We rejoice every time we see a harbour porpoise, and the first of the season is always a party to celebrate. It is duly noted in the log at night, so that I can reread and relive the big joys in the little things in the comfort of my armchair during the winter.

Birds, ships, other boats, to greet and be greeted not to mention sailing close to a coast enjoying its distinct contours and landscapes. A heron in a corner of Svendborg Sound near Troense, which we always check out, or the cows on a hillside at the island Bjørnø, which I circumnavigate frequently.

My son Emil the proud fisherman after catching a Garfish. That was truly a great micro adventure for all the kids involved. About half an hour after the picture was taken, the fish was prepared and fried in butter on the ship's stove.

The shallower the draft of the pocket cruiser, the more possibilities we have for getting close to coastal nature experiences. Several small ports become accessible, that are otherwise denied to boats of more than 1.0-1.2 metres draft. You can explore shallow waters usually unattainable (with due consideration for protected nesting areas of birds and wildlife). For a large part, Danish inland waters (the Baltic Sea) are for the majority rather shallow, so the world becomes significantly bigger for the smallest of sailboats.

I remember when my son caught a garfish in the middle of a fresh force 5 sailing trip. Later, when safely moored it was the most amazing experience for the five children aboard to skin, clean and fry the fish and sharing it in five small portions.

When lying in port with children aboard the best micro adventures are often catching crabs and the tiny ill tempered eel pouts, playing with them in a bucket before releasing them back into their natural habitat again. If we join them in their activity, it will also become an adult micro adventure. It is a privilege that we are allowed to experience the little wonders of nature, wher ever we encounter them.

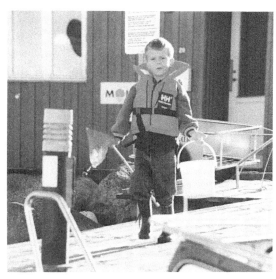

Catching crabs in a fishing net is an instant adventure for every child when lying in port.

Visiting the numerous small islands of the Sourthern Funen Archipelago is a micro adventure, where you feel the clock has been turned backwards to the 1950's, and where a personal adventure of mine is to check that a simple farm house lamp is still in its place on the fasade of a farm in the middle of the village at Lyø island.

Mette wasn't particularly keen on visiting the small island Hjortø. Only 6 people live there in each their farmhouse and the tiny harbour only offers cold running water, a toilet and electricity for visiting yachts. However, she was overly enthusiastic, when we managed to observe one of the very rare fire-bellied toads. I still recall the tranquility and beauty on a beach by the reef, where we sat and enjoyed reading a book.

Micro adventures have both meditative qualities such as indulging or immersing yourself in something, be it purely experiencing or of an augmenting natural presence. It is both healthy mindfulness, recreational and an experience. Wikipedia is your friendly travel companion. A wealth of interesting knowledge at hand, where ever we have mobile coverage.

Many years ago, my friend Jørn and I visited the island Samsø in Kattegat on our first cruise together with our two little boys in the Hurley 20 Tulle. We visited the minute Kyholm museum in Ballen and witnessed two old blokes in soldiers' uniforms from the 1850's giving a cannon salute. We visited Nordby by bus and got lost in the spruce forest labyrinth and followed in the foot steps of the vikings along the Kanhave canal. The highlight being resting for our lunch in the fields and a bull following us with only a most questionable wire fence between us.

It is a quite extraordinary experience of enjoyment to be able to drop anchor and eat a foodpack or anchor for the night in a place free from any manmade sounds - on your own or in the company of a dear friend. The silence is an adventure in itself.

Underway I sometimes close my eyes and feel the wind by turning my head from side to side, sensing the warmth or the chill, feeling the rain dripping on me or how I gradually get dry and warm again in the sun.

Also the lonely trips in the after season, where it gets really dark and chilly at night, can be an adventure. Often there are but a few other living souls in the ports in late August or September. There is no better reward after a fresh and even tough passage than getting into port, clearing up down below, putting the heat on, taking off your shoes and curling up in a bunk. And then expectantly enjoying the smell of your supper simmering on the stove, while you reflect on the day's sail and the day to follow. I love these moments; letting the silence be replaced by a piece of jazz or classical music on my bluetooth loudspeaker, letting tiredness be replaced by the gratitude of feeling full after a meal and a glass of wine.

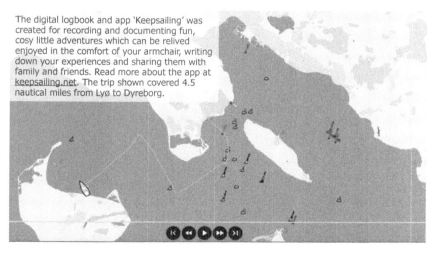

The digital logbook and app 'Keepsailing' was created for recording and documenting fun, cosy little adventures which can be relived enjoyed in the comfort of your armchair, writing down your experiences and sharing them with family and friends. Read more about the app at keepsailing.net. The trip shown covered 4.5 nautical miles from Lyø to Dyreborg.

On the first outing of the season, I notice how the boat heels over for in a gust of wind and how it reacts by charging forward with just light pressure on the tiller, accelerating from 1.5 to 3 knots and then suddenly 5-5.5 knots.

The quirking sounds from rig and sails vibrantly and enthusiastically telling me that she is in her element and just cannot wait to take off. Every year I need to get my sealegs back and use the first outing to get accustomed to the boat's movements.

Come autumn, the days get shorter and the evenings pitch black and a micro adventure can be reading a book in the shelter of the sprayhood from the cold wind, feeling the warming signs that the sun is still in power, a life giving cup of coffee underway and having a good talk with my crew. Not to mention a heartening sandwich down below after putting into port and clearing up the ship.

Part of the philosophy of the micro adventure is to find it in the seemingly insignificant.

My son Oscar also wanted to go on an adventure with his dad and the autumn holiday included an overnight adventure onboard safely moored. We read a bunktime story in candle light and crept under a few layers of blankets into our sleeping bags and enjoyed a wonderful micro adventure. Getting to experience adventures seen through the eyes of small children is truly a gift. And just as fond a memory for me today as it was for him.

3. WHY SMALL IS GREAT

Small craft are easily managed. When having an overview, you get the sensation of being able to master the little beast. Also contributing to the overview is simplicity. The less you fill up your boat with, the better it can be managed. Economy adds to the overview. Small sailboats are often quite cheap to acquire and more apt to be used with cheaper alternatives to expensive marina berths or moorings like mud berths or stationed on a trailer. Sails are cheaper. Antiifouling paint, cleansing and polishing articles and all that goes along with maintenance are proportionally more affordable. Insurance can also be a lot less costly.

I favour the idea of a boat you "can wear;" as an expression of feeling at one with your boat, sensing its motion in the swell and through the water. The idea that your boat becomes a small container of your whole world, where you have everything you need within reach. There is profound sustainability and healthy condition in maintaining a certain degree of self-sufficiency; food, roof over your head, a warm berth, as well as the wind and modest quantity of petrol to take you, where ever you wish to go. Keep turning to port and you will eventually circumnavigate the globe or your local small island. And you can do it even in the smallest of crafts. But you will also be able to experience the adventure right in front of you, just outside the harbour. Entrusted with yourself under the grace of weather and wind.

Manageable

When mooring, you can fender off with your hands or haul you and the boat forward with the help of poles and guiding lines in a tight spot. Even the smallest outboard can push a small sailboat with ease. There are no heavy things or need for strong muscle in a tiny boat. On a 27 foot sailboat however, the big genoa alone is rather heavy when folded and packed in its sailbag.

This is very different in smaller boats. The spring cleaning and preparation is less time consuming and demanding. Fewer square metres to clean, polish, wax and paint. Heating down below can be narrowed down to lighting the stove for 10 minutes with a lovely snug warm boat as a result. You can take it out of the water yourself in many places, using a self-serviced crane and towing it on a trailer. Low draft also makes it possible to beach it and wade on shore. A smaller anchor is also good for your backside. Sitting down below, you can reach almost anything from your position in the middle of the cabin. Mistakes are punished less severely and with manageable consequences still contributing to your learning experience.

Little people will have a positive experience, when they realise, that they can master a small sailboat. Small sailboats are quite simply more at eye-level for children; they can fish with a fishing net and bathe from the boat. Every rope or line to haul require less effort than on bigger boats.

Sailing should be for every one

It ought to be financially and humanly affordable for every one to go sailing. With lots of small old boats in the market it is more than ever a sport for the common man, and there is a renaissance tendency. Free boats and cheap boats everywhere. Often a bit stale and neglected, but rubbing beneath the sad surface, letting the high pressure cleaner and polish do their bit, genuine little gems reveal themselves as sleeping beauties, waiting for the love of their second life and rescuer and for new hope and glory. Often elbow-grease and a modest budget will get you at sea in a boat, in which you can be happy and enjoy many lovely experiences.

"At sea I learned,
how little a man needs.
Not how much"
- unknown

4. SAILING ON A SMALL BUDGET

The whole purpose of this book is to explain, how I accomplished to get lots of sailing experiences and learn a lot on a small budget without compromising the fun of it.

Throughout the history of pleasure boating the richest people set the standard for what to sail and how to sail it. Concurrently ordinary people made great effort to also gain access to the attractive sailing scene.

In the 1850's it became more and more commonplace to sail for fun and to race. Only the richest people could afford the new sport. It was hardly an off hours spare time activity, as they had no work to hold them from sailing. Sailing was merely a distraction.

Around 1900 workers in the cities began to have leisure time, and among them people, who also fancied a pastime at sea. They attempted to race their double ended "krage-dinghies," traditional Danish open workboats, that any boatbuilder could build on the beach by rule of thumb. Yardsticks were attempted but never really worked properly. It was however the first popular movement in terms of getting people with ordinary income out sailing.

In 1926 a yardstick and design competition for a "Class double ender" is held, which results in the building of the first renowned Danish class double enders. Three designers dominated the classes: Aage Utzon (the father of Jørn Utzon, the architect of Sydney Opera House), M.S.J. Hansen and Georg Berg. Class double enders were built right up until 1970, and they were a popular success. Throughout the country, many boats were built on the beach in small boat guilds of two or three men, and in this way people with ordinary modest income could become boat owners. This was the second attempt of the common man to find his way to sea.

With the appearance of glassfibre reinforced plastic or GRP as building material in the 1960's it became even more affordable to become a boat owner and making one's wet dreams come true. Wages became an ever more essential part of the building costs, so industrial serial production made good sense. Workers' after hours increased and demands soared. This was the third wave of the common man's attempt to go to sea.

The welfare death spiral dictated a newer and ever bigger boat as inflation and buying power made it possible, until the financial crisis in 2009 hit. Boats had always been a relatively safe investment and suddenly many boats were in fact worthless or dropped in value to a fraction of the former price level. Today we find ourselves in the situation, where boat owners may give their boat away for free, or you only have to pay a symbolic price for a boat, that a few years ago would have cost real money. Of course you have to be prepared to invest in a free boat to be properly seaworthy or outfitted, but the truth is, that is has never been more affordable to become a boat owner than now. The way to sea has in deed been paved for anyone wanting to go sailing.

So much so that today it is being discussed, whether owning things has a value in itself nor if it is even desirable? Do you have to own your boat? Couldn't you just lend, rent or share? You can do it in all the ways, I mentioned. My passion for sailing was never about big expensive yachts, rather their opposites; the small modest and often neglected gems, that will give their owners their full payoff for their modest cost.

Minimalism has a special capability. Just how small can you sail and still find it meaningful and rewarding, creating joy and contentment? The answer is as small, as you like. Open or half decked daysailers can be great cruising boats on a camping comfort level and in relatively sheltered waters. The smallest of pocket cruisers of say 16-18 feet can be a hearty luxury and extravagant freedom for a solo sailor or two, who love each other. And you only have to step up one class to 22-24 feet to find boats with family potential.

Here is a calculated example based on Danish conditions in 2020 prices show the annual grand total of owning a small boat based on modest investments and renewal of sails with good second hand ones:

Marina berth	700 €
Liability insurance	130 €
Maintenance	300 €
Launching and haul out	130 €
Annual budget	1,260 €

If you still think that 105 € a month is a lot of money, find two or three mates to share the pleasure and work with, and you will be sailing for the price of a few café lattes or an evening in the cinema. This way you will always have someone to sail with and someone to have tea or coffee with at 13 cents a cup, when you cook it on the stove on board.

Even students can join in, and why postpone your dreams until after your graduation, after the kids have grown bigger, or you have paid the mortgage on your new garage?

Go small. Go sailing. Go now.

Another option is to rent a boat. It may cost a little more per sailing trip, but if you don't use your boat very much apart from a holiday cruise and the occasional outing, it makes good sense to rent a boat, which is also kept seaworthy and properly maintained. In this way many sailors share the same resource, and you don't have a lot of money or negative emotional capital tied up in a sailboat, to grow a guilty conscience, creating pressure and stress. An additional advantage worth mentioning, is that you are not limited to your own boat but get to sail others throughout a season.

I have sailed my entire life on a modest budget and have followed at least three different strategies, reflecting temperament, ambition and conditions, which you can read about in the following chapter.

5. CHOICE OF PHILOSOPHY AND STRATEGY

Start by choosing your philosophy and strategy. What are your sailing and boat life goals?

Strategy number 1: Sail cheap now and for as long as you can

You could buy a boat in a reasonable condition and run it financially lowkey, where you don't improve its condition but profit from its solidity and general sound condition. The aim is to get as much enjoyment out of sailing it, as the modest budget allows without any actual improvements.

When we bought our Spækhugger (as a boat sharing community for two and later three), this was our strategy. We formulated it somewhat likes this; it is not our goal to own anything, so we shall just keep the investment relatively intact (that was before the financial crisis and massive drop in boat prices). We will therefore not pay off the boat but simply cover the interest and direct minimum costs. Our budget was 35 € a month, until an osmosis repair became necessary after a couple of years. We enjoyed a lot of great cruises and outings in this boat.

Strategy number 2: Safeguard your money and sail well

Or you could regard your purchase as an investment, where you buy a boat, which is somewhat better for the price, you must pay for it. Presumably a slightly smaller boat or with less equipment and in a better condition. By investing a little every season or replacing things, you care for your investment and always have a boat in good shape as well as a source of joy and worry free sailing.

When we bought an old 22 ft. Marsvin, which had seen a lot of racing in its day and had several soft spots on deck and coachroof, the strategy was to invest in more comfort and enjoy the quite good sails it came equipped with. Over a period of six to seven years we invested more than 3,000 € in improvements and made a partial structural repair when cutting up the sandwich construction in the coachroof around the mast to take away rotten balsa wood and relaminating it with plywood, which was more work than investment. The result reinforced the boat rather well but only constituted a partial repair. But throughout the seven years of ownership, we were sailing well and each year on a slightly better level.

Strategy number 3: Whatever you do, do it properly

You can also choose to see your modest initial investment as a good outset for being able to sail on a continously satisfactory level and an affordable budget. Put a little money aside every month to afford changing a sail one year and berth cushions the next etc.

With this investment philosophy, we bought our 27 ft. Grinde yacht in 2016. We invested 22,000 € in a well maintained sailboat from 1975, known to defy the market tendency by keeping its market value. Furthermore it was extravagantly equipped, so we used the sale of excessive equipment the first year to finance several improvements. The boat is a community with two parties, each paying 200 € a month with a calculated capital of 2,800 € a year for maintenance, servicing and replacements. In two years we managed to acquire a new foresail and new cabin mattresses and a series of smaller improvements; spring clamps on the rubrail, an expensive quality anchor etc.

In practice, there need not be a huge difference between the three strategies. If you buy a Spækhugger for instance, you can sail it hard and wear on its solidity, without deteriorating it very much over a shorter time span, while other boats perhaps won't take the same brutal use. A solid built boat can always be rebuilt later, but it is a lot cheaper and more satisfactory to take on the maintenance and repair tasks, as they occur and be on top of the decay. All boats will detoriorate without tender loving care, and I do not favour a use-and-throw-away-mentality in pleasure boating. On the contrary.

We ought to regard the sailboats we are trusted with at symbolic low prices or even given, as something we eventually pass on to others. Some sort of added value will mean, that every one is winning, whether or not money is exchanged, or if it is a gesture of pure philanthropy.

Important questions you should ask yourself

What do you want from your boat, and how much does it matter to you? What does it mean for you to have it? How would you like to use it? How much money are you willing to spend on it, and what can you afford? Do you have the support of your partner? On what level do you wish to sail?

I once lent a boat to a sailor, who was overly enthusiastic about the venture but did not match his expectations with his girlfriend. A month after having sailed the boat to his home port, he had to cancel our agreement, because he did not have her support. However much I understood and appreciated his situation, it also was a sign of not having thought through the consequences of realising his dream. Happiness isn't always to have ones dreams come true.

On our current shared sailboat, we accept, that things break or wear. The boat is built and bought to be used, and our strategy is not to be overly cautious but to take good care of things, while we use them and replace them when they fail or break. In this way we always have a boat in good working condition, which is a delight to sail.

6. CHOOSE A GOOD BOAT

I imagine, that you are interested in the absolutely most financially affordable model, and then we work ourselves towards boats requiring a larger initial investment and maintenance. A rule of thumb is that the bigger the boat, the more expensive everything for it will be, and the more equipment could break or fail. And for that reason the bigger boat ought to be in a generally better condition.

> The joy of sailing is inversely proportional
> to the size of the boat.

The formulay is an agreed creed between us pocket cruiser-skippers. Not that I wouldn't appreciate sailing a big well functioning 40 footer, but my joy of ownership and of sailing it would be ruined by installments resembling those of a house. I cannot afford two houses. So even if I have all sorts of strong opinions regarding why I chose the Grinde as my boat, my personal formula for the joy of sailing really is: anything that floats.

Good sailing characteristics

Once you have found your boat, you should get to know it and how to sail it on its terms and with respect for your crew's. All sailboats are a sum of compromises and a set of different characteristics. Don't listen to those, who equal windward capacity and speed as being the criteria for good sailing characteristics. There are far more parameters. The boat's motion in a swell is an interaction between displacement, hullform and beam as well as the mast height and sail area.

Through many years of studying our ship's log, I have come to the conclusion, that we can count on a progress of 4 knots on average in force 2-4 airs and 5 knots in force 5 and above. This means, that in the course of a daysail of 6

Foreground: Hurley 18, in the middle a Hurley 22 and in the background a Carina 20

hours, we cover 24 respectively 30 nautical miles. Calculate your planned distance in the side of your seachart with a ruler: 1 lattitude minute = 1 nautical mile. Divide by your average sail speed. Then you have your estimated sailing time in hours.

6 x 3.5 knots = 21 nautical miles
6 x 4.0 knots = 24 nautical miles
6 x 4.5 knots = 27 nautical miles
6 x 5.0 knots = 30 nautical miles

A satisfying speed range depending on the boat size may range between 3.5 and 5 knots, when we look at older traditional cruising boats. As we for metheorological and landscape dependent reasons often encounter a headwind along the coasts, a sailboat ought to work its way to windward satisfactory. The term is "velocity made good" and includes the speed towards and from the wind. In this case the optimal relationship between speed and accomplished angle to the wind covering the distance over ground. Most sailboats perform best in force 4 to 5. In light airs it gets difficult for some boats and in gale force wind for most boats, if both wind, swell and current run against them.

In our Hurley 18 and Hurley 20 we have tacked easily and effortlessly with old sails, not making more than maybe 50^0 to windward. But if you don't attempt to push it to do 45^0 to windward, it sails effortlessly well. Good sails are directly connected to good sailing characteristics. The jib is the most important sail, when it comes to gaining windward progress, speed while tacking and less heeling. The balance in a boat is probably one of the most important aspects of the pleasure of sailing. A sailboat which is constantly hard on the helm is no joy and rather straneous. This is the responsibilty of the designer. The rest is about your expertise in balancing sails and trim.

A good cruising yacht has a soft movement in a swell. Heavy boats with a well designed bow have an advantage. Generally you can say, that light displacement sailboats demand more of their skipper in terms of experience. However, they offer other advantages being trailerable.

Comfort in a small boat

Besides sailing characteristics, a series of things contribute to create comfort in a small boat. Let's start on the foredeck. It should be easy to move across the deck from bow to stern. Many small boats pose challenges in this area. The side deck should be wide enough to put one's foot down with a little to spare. If that is not possible, it is often intended, that you tread across the coachroof. A large pultpit in the bow is nice to have but also a barrier to overcome for the less experienced, when getting safely to and from the jetty. A searail is a convenience and could improve safety, but it is not strong enough in itself and should not be trusted. But it adds to the feeling, that you can move about safely while moored in port.

The cockpit should be designed for good sitting comfort, so that you will sit well. It is probably one of the most important points, as you spend most of the time aboard in the cockpit. If it also offers good lying comfort, consider it an added bonus. With kapok cushions you can make a nice back rest and also sit on comfort while under way. The variant made from coconut fibres is just as practical and durable yet not entirely as comfortable. If you can find room for a couple of boat seats with adjustable backrests, it will be a small luxury improving any boat.

Down below seating comfort is equally important, as most pocket cruisers don't offer standing headroom. And you do spend a lot of the time onboard sitting. Is it bad weather or cold, you ought to be able to endure sitting below reading, having a cup of tea, eating and socializing. One of the main arguments for buying a pocket cruiser over a much larger boat is, that the space below is bought at a high cost, when most sailors don't spend any time below except when sleeping. But in my opinion the living accomodations are vastly overlooked as a quality in sailing your own little boat. Sitting comfort also include back rest, being able to sit up without bowing your neck, where the deck joins the coachroof.

"The cabin of a small yacht is truly a wonderful thing;
not only will it shelter you from a tempest,
but for the other troubles in life,
it is a safe retreat"
- Francis Herreshoff

According to their brochures, most of even the smallest boats offer four berths but in practice room for two + potentially a couple of children. 17-18 ft. boats offer a cruising capacity for two adults or one adult and a couple of children for sailors, who will accept simple camping comfort. The berths should have proper length. And you should bring a measuring tape if looking at a potential boat, as many boats are fitted with rather too short berths. The beam ought to be 50 cm or more, and the headroom of quarter berths high enough to be able sleep on the side or turn while lying in your sleeping bag. Quarter berths are often used for stowing gear and clothes. Two examples of quarter berths from my personal experience: In the Spækhugger (24 ft.) you can hardly turn in the quarter berth, whereas one can actually sit up in the quarter berth of the Marsvin (22 ft.). Equally the Hurley 18 offers a rather high and spacious quarter berth.

In general you should not expect standing headroom on a pocket cruiser. Only few boats below 25-26 ft. offer standing headroom, but in my research I did find a couple of exceptions to the rule with real standing headroom (170-180 cm): Hurley 24/700, Polaris Drabant 26 and surprisingly also Leisure 22 and 23. Look for details in the boat type section in Chapter 14 with approximate headroom, where I have been able to acquire the data.

Is standing headroom important for comfort? Most men would probably not think so, but if they have the ambition to enlist their wifes and sweethearts, then they will realize, that they often consider it important. One end of the scale would be "standing headroom" and the opposite could consequently be referred to as "sitting headroom." In a Hurley 18 you can just sit up, but the boat and especially the cabin floor is so short, that it doesn't matter really.

The Spækhugger offers approximately 120 cm sitting headroom under the coachroof, but the boat is rather longer with its 24 ft., and "sitting headroom" + "crawling headroom" is the more fitting description of this particular boat, which takes some getting used to when moving fore and aft below deck. But what would be the fitting term for the cross between sitting and standing headroom? The Marsvin offers a generous 140 cm. Enough "standing headroom" for putting on a pair of trousers while standing, and the distance between the forecastle and cabin is so short, that it doesn't seem inhibiting. I would recommend anything above 140 cm as a really good compromise.

Heating

In a pocket cruiser it is hardly realistic to fit in a diesel heater, which is a luxury heating source, but in small boats any source will count including the warmth of a companion. Under way the possibility to get a hot cup of tea or coffee is almost a lifesaving heat source. Fill a couple of thermos flasks before departure. Nothing boosts morale and endurance like a nice cup of tea or soup, and even more so on a long tough passage leg, when the weather surprises you from its less favourable side. By lighting the stove, which is often times based on alcohol, gas or kerosene, you heat the cold below quarters in an instant, so that you can take turns to go below and get warmed up. A catalyst or alcohol stove for heating is an efficient and cheap way of heating your boat, but remember to keep the hatch open to vent the exhaust fumes and only when moored! We have an alcohol stove onboard but never use it overnight. A Refleks or Dickinson stove is a real ships stove, which can be mounted with a through-deck flue pipe and fuelled with diesel, only using electricity when igniting. It's a great but pricy solution. It can be quite cold at night in the early season, so adding a couple of woollen blankets to a good quality sleeping bag is generally a good idea for cold spring nights. On our summer cruise we sleep with light summer duvets.

The psychological effect of warmth onboard is a pleasant sense of safety and security for the less experienced crew.

Water

You can easily install a water tank onboard with a water tap and a mechanical or electrical pump. But basically you don't need a fixed installation, which adds to the complexity of things, needs maintenance and could break.

The simplest water supply onboard is a 5-10 litre plastic canister or camping canister and a couple of 2 litre pet bottles of super market still water. Easy to refill and tap from. But how much water do you need a day? Of course this is quite individual, but in our experience from a small camping canister over the seasons we use 15 litres a day on average. Water is important for avoiding dehydration under way but obviously also for laundry, cooking and doing the dishes.

Electrical installations

The electrical installations are a weak point in most older boats. Often undocumented, not complying to regulatory standards and rebuilt and extended over 30-50 years. Many new boat owners take the consequence and rip it all out once and for all to renew the lot with new cables in the right dimensions and a new switch panel. Consult an experienced boat owner or professional literature on the subject if in doubt. Bad electrical installations present a safety hazard. The boat's batteries primarily run a few instruments and lighting. For that purpose a battery of 75-110 AH will do nicely. Remember! By all means do switch to LED below decks but stick to the old type of navigation light bulbs for your mast top, as LED bulbs are much too strong for comfort for fellow sailors to be a good replacement. I speak of personal experience and found the LED lights of other boats most annoying during a yacht race at night a couple of years ago. And when using LED bulbs below deck, make sure they are shielded from radio noise.

The more instruments you have onboard, the more amps you will need from your batteries. On the other hand you would do just as well with a seachart, a ruler and a handbearing compass (in your binoculars). That is how I navigate currently - with a Navionics navigation app on my iPhone and iPad. They have a battery life of one sailing day when fully charged. A small solar panel could make you independent of the electrical naval chord and expensive marinas, while being able to anchor for days. Be aware, that having electrical extension chords attached to shore installations for longer periods incur the risk of galvanic corrosion of all under water metal like propeller and propeller-shaft etc.

Toilet - bucket or porta potti?

A vital safety factor onboard is how you are able to relieve yourself, when the urge is compelling. The combination of wind, water and cold may expedite the need. Should the boat be fitted with a separate toilet, or is it sufficient with one under the forecastle v-berth? A bucket is not only a great life insurance, if the boat leaks, but also for peeing, when you cannot access a toilet. We sailed our 22 ft. Marsvin for a couple of years with only a bucket in the cockpit, which we emptied over the side. It worked fine, but my wife was very happy, when we got ourselves a porta potti toilet, which we stowed under the companionway and pulled out on the cabin floor when needed.

When single handed, it requires some disregard for death to hold onto the shroud with one hand and steer one's thingy with the other and pee over the side. The rule for moving safely about onboard is:

One hand for the ship and one for yourself!

If you allow young and old boys to pee over the side, you might use my self invented command, with which I used to have my boys playfully learn the habit of awarenes and attention not to fall overboard: "Standby to piss!" The reply should be rehearsed as: "Ready to piss!"

A separate heads in a boat below 30 ft. is often a cramped closet, in which you reverse with the trousers pulled down first. It is far better to have it in the cabin and pay attention to preserve the modesty and dignity of the crew. You are very close in the confined space of a little ship. Most crews will accept a main rule formulated like this: Small aboard and big ashore! And the emergency rule to break it: If you have to, you must! Portable toilets and a bucket are simple, do not require through-hull installations and practically cannot break up. But seawater toilets and holding tanks can, and they are a step away from simple and safe.

Choose a boat built in high numbers

If you choose a boat that has been built in larger numbers, there probably is a better documentation of the construction, an owners association and access to the knowledge collected and the history of the boat as well as potential answers to technical questions.

Boats like Hurley 18, Leisure 17, Marieholm 20, Drabant 22, Junker 22, Carina 20, LM22, Marieholm Seacat, Stortriss and L23 etc. are boats, that can be purchased for anything between 800-3,000 €. The closer you get to 800 € in 2020 money, the more we are speaking of a boat, that may be in a healthy state but also in need of both tender loving care and a bit of reinvestment. Often it may be a fully workable sailboat but in need of interior restoration, though otherwise intact. But you can also be in luck and make a real bargain in the lower end of the price range. The closer you get to 3,000 €, the more will probably already have been improved, renewed or reinvested, and maybe there is even an outboard engine in good condition.

The point is, that if the boat is structurally in order and not in need of major repairs or comprehensive refurbishment, it will surely be worth more in usability and lasting value than the price you will have to pay for it, if you maintain it conscientiously until it is passed on to its next owner.

Don't write off the rare or special boats in advance

The counter strategy could be choosing the opposite of boats built in large numbers. Boats that for commercial reasons didn't make it in the market, could very well be a great buy and stir up attention, when you sail it. They might offer an interesting history and possess a different value than sheer market dominance.

Ask for guidance from an experienced boat owner or marine surveyor

Regardless of which dreamboat, you are contemplating, expect that the years won't have gone by without trace. We are speaking of GRP boats from the 1960's and 70's, and 40-50 years is an advanced age for a boat, if it hasn't been kept properly or endured alterations without the necessary boat building skills. For that reason you will need someone to accompany you, who isn't already in love and may view the ship with critical realism. If you don't have a person with these skills in your network, get professional help and regard it as part of your investment.

Also, remember that sailors are often biased by their subjective beliefs and experience, and they are not the ones, who will buy, own and sail the boat in question. You are. Their advice may be influenced by their own preferences, and they may differ from yours in relation to what the ideal boat should look like. So take their advice and make an independent decision of your own. Your skipper's training begins right here, right now. It is your choice and your responsibility.

In my experience there is no such thing as the perfect boat. The best compromise between an array of important properties is really, what we should consider.

If you are thinking more about a boat in which you can grow the interest and bring along both family or friends, it is worth looking at good buys in the 24-26 foot class, with more elbow room and minimum four real full length berths, where you will also encounter tougher conditions with a sizeable reassuring displacement.

Here you have a handful of selected genuine classics giving all Danish sailors above 50 affectionate longing associations, no matter what boat they may sail today: Drabant 22, Spækhugger, Bandholm 24, Nordic Folkboat and the International Folkboat.

7. ADVICE ON BUYING A 30-50 YEAR OLD BOAT

Purchasing a low budget pocket cruiser from a marine surveyor's perspective

by Uwe Gräfer, Marine surveyor at Hanse Sportboot-Sachverständige in Hamburg.

The market for brokerage in general

The market situation for second hand boats of a certain age (30 years or even older) is beneficial for buyers. There are lots of bargains and good buys available. The initial conclusion: There is no need to be in a hurry and certainly no reason to take on a wreck, even if you can get it for free.

Marinas abound with small boats waiting for tender loving care. The question is, whether they are a find or a wreck. One should pay attention to this and not be in a hurry.

Many boats are at the end of their realistic life span, and the owner could just be looking for an opportunity to save the costs of having it scrapped. The cost of scrapping a 6 m. boat in Scandinavia could easily be 1,300 €. So be careful not to fall into that trap. Look for boats in good condition. There are plenty of those around.

Safety should prevail

Even if you plan to buy a low cost pocket cruiser, you are hardly willing to risk the lives of your family and friends. The boat must be safe and worthy of the sea. How safe depends on your sailing agenda: Do you plan to daysail on a shallow lake or in protected coastal waters? Or do you dream of crossing the Kattegat and visit the Swedish skerries or even an Atlantic crossing to the Caribean?

Many pocket cruisers are safe constructions, and some have survived real adventures in the high seas. But material fatigue, insufficient maintenance or bad repairs may have weakened an otherwise solid design.

Basic prepurchase checkpoints

Hull / Keel / Rudder

The hull most be water tight, unless we are speaking about a wooden planker built boat. Plywood boats like Bohème and Waarschip should also be dry. If a GRP boat is leaking, there is a problem. Don't trust an owner's assurance, that it is minor question of condensation or humidity. Maybe the keel and hull joint is leaking, or the through-hull seacocks are corroded. Seacocks are a minor problem, as they are easily replaced. Loose keelbolts are a bigger issue. Examine them carefully, while the boat is in the water and while sailing. If the boat has an inboard engine, additional items need to be checked in terms of leaks. Spray the deck and coachroof with a water hose to check for leaks in windows, hatches and the deck. Believe me: A wet berth isn't much fun.

The rudder blade, rudder stock, gudgeon and pintle are of decisive significance. If these parts fail, your boat will be in serious trouble. Look for loose parts, play in the rudder bushings, cracks, rot in the tiller and a weak rudder blade.

Osmosis is a general concern for GRP hulls and rudder. You can look for visible blisters, when the boat has just been taken out of the water. If it stood on the dry for long, you can't actually see it. If the osmosis condition is visible, the structural entity of the hull is endangered. The boat will not exactly break down in pieces, but the stability of the laminate will have deteriorated. The bottom will start to become soft, and the keel section may start to become moveable etc.

Trailer boats often display stress marks at the supporting points on the trailer. Look for cracks, scratches and "play" in the hull, when someone is walking about the boat when resting on the trailer.

Rig and sail

The mast, boom and standing rigging are apart from the sails the true engine of the sailboat. You must be able to trust these items! Check mast and boom for sign of galvanic corrosion (corrosion caused by contact between aluminium and stainless steel parts), cracks in stress points (like spreaders) and deformation. The mast as such must be in good condition, as new mast fittings are quite expensive and often require some adapting and adjustments.

The standing rigging (shrouds and stays of steel wire) isn't difficult to replace. If these parts exceed more than 15-20 years, professional riggers recommend considering a replacement. The costs for 6 m. boat would amount to approximately 350 €.

The running rigging isn't a safety issue but more of a comfort matter. Invest in dyneema halyards, and you will add both comfort of sailing and much improved performance. Blocks and winches are easily serviced or replaced. You can expect to find great bargains on Ebay or similar platforms.

The sails ought to be in a reasonably good condition without immediate need of repairs. In this way you get to choose yourself, whether you would rather spend a lot of money in a sailloft or be patient and find a good used sail on the internet. Your mainsail ought to have reefs for reducing the sail area in an increasing wind. The foresail wardrobe should include a jib in a heavier fabric, if you don't have a furling genoa. But even then it is convenient to have an extra jib, if problems should occur with the genoa or furling gear.

Engine

As I mentioned earlier, the sail wardrobe is your actual engine. A pocket cruiser can be maneuvered under sail and with muscular power in 95% of all sailing situations and under most conditions. But most of us seek comfort: An engine is nice to have, if the wind dies out, or the marina is narrow and cramped.

Most pocket cruisers are equipped with petrol driven outboard engines. A two-stroke engine is noisy, thirsty and smelly but has the advantage of a comparably lower weight. It eases handling and improves the weight trim of the boat.

Four stroke engines are less noisy, more fuel efficient and have a pleasant engine dynamic but at the cost of a larger weight.

In both instances you should check the ignition and running culture of the engine. If it is water cooled (which applies to most engines), you should be able to see a small stream of water coming out of the engine leg. It indicates, that the water pump is working as intended, and that the engine is cooling. Give it a „test run," and force it into high revolutions. It should be able to do that without any problems. If not, then plan to have it serviced by a mechanic or replaced. A used 5 hp (4-stroke) outboard could cost between 400 and 700 €. Older two-stroke engines are often times cheaper.

Inboard petrol or diesel engines require more attention. Check for oil spillage in the sump below the engine, smell of diesel or petrol. Propeller and propeller shaft shouldn't show signs of corrosion: There must be a zinc anode fitted to prevent corrosion, and the propeller shaft rubber sleeve for the shaft bearing should be dry. While running, no visible smoke should be seen from the exhaust. Blue exhaust fumes indicate a higher oil consumption, unless it is a two stroke inboard engine. White exhaust fumes is a sign of insufficient cooling or a leaking head gasket. Black exhaust fumes from diesel engines may come from injection pump problems.

In any case: Old engines from discontinued brands may cause a lot of problems with getting spare parts. So if you might be facing problems with such an engine, replacing it with an outboard instead could be a solution.

8. TRAILER OR MARINA BERTH

If you choose a smaller boat with a swing keel or centerplate with a total weight less than 1,000 kg, you could easily trail it with a medium sized car and launch it from a slip or a self-serviced swing crane. Thus you will spare the costs for a marina berth or mooring.

In some places marina berths are difficult to get as well as the biggest single cost in a small sailboat budget. So much speaks for storing the boat on a trailer ready to launch and sail, thereby only paying for the days, you actually sail. By far most sailboats remain in harbour for 90% of the time, while their owners toil at work to pay for the boat, or they are away at Mallorca or in a summer house or at the golf course. In short, a boat is a really expensive pleasure measured by hours spent sailing. You should probably not make that calculation. Think about getting yourself a trailer instead.

You could pack your car and trailer and go on a Thursday afternoon after work and reach Gothenburg or Stockholm and enjoy a sailing weekend in parts of Europe or even corners of your native waters normally out of reach during a three week summer cruise. Endless opportunities, if you think small, far and right here and now.

However, a permanent marina berth holds other amenity values in store. Even the smallest of boats will also be a cosy little floating summer house with exchangeable seaview, where you go and enjoy yourself, spend a night or make outings in the local waters. The summer cruise will be limited by, how far you can sail out and back in 2-3 weeks. If you wish to extend your operating radius, have a friend borrow your boat and hand over the baton at your destination, for him or her to sail it back over the next weeks. Or find a good place to keep the boat for a while at a reasonable cost and sail it back over the next few weekends, enabling you to attend to your work duties in between. Thinking outside of the box will render lots of different possibilities.

If you are lucky enough to choose between more marinas, you should check the ambience of the marina and sense, if you would enjoy staying there, when you are not sailing. Are there fine cruising destinations in reach from your home port, and how far must you sail to reach other detinations? Check the terms and conditions for hauling out and keeping your boat on land during the winter. Prices may vary quite a lot as well as terms and conditions from one marina to the next, like rules for keeping the mast standing or being forced to derig the mast. I have experienced broken navigation lights and windex, because other boat owners crashed or ruined things while carrying their masts in and out of the common mast shed. An unnecessary cost and quite annoying too.

9. MAINTENANCE AND REPAIR

One must possess quite a few competencies as a boat owner, but do not despair in advance. It can be learned, and one of the pleasures of owning a boat is, that you acquire many useful skills along the way.

I usually say, that as a skipper and boat owner, you have to be a fairly competent craftsman: Electrician; plummer; mechanic and sailmaker. You should be able to cook and at least make coffee and sandwiches, navigate, sail, be a good leader and a bit of a psychologist on occasion. Most sailors take their sailing very seriously and each one has his or her particular view on, how things are done in an appropriate way and are willing to discuss it at lengths with those of a different opinion. There are many right ways to do things, and when you are sitting out there on the water wondering about the solution to a problem, you should try to ask yourself and find your own solutions rather than posing your question on facebook first or making Google your best friend. You strengthen your self reliance by working it out and by accepting, that out there you are completely and utterly left to your own devices. And that is quite literally part of the charm.

On land the boat needs to be spring and autumn cleaned and prepared, polished, antifouled, repaired and looked after. Many years ago, Politiken published the book "I am a Sailor" (in Danish), which I read back and forth over and over again at the age of fourteen. I highly recommend similar books about learning to sail and everything maritime. In your local marina you can learn a lot from fellow sailors from ingenious tips to good alternative products, that do the job at a fraction of the cost. Everything labelled "maritime" or "yacht" cost far more than equivalent landbased products for maintenance and cleaning. I don't mean to belittle their obvious excellence but rather keep my focus on cost minimisation.

10. SECOND HAND AS FIRST CHOICE

For small craft you will find a vast selection of used equipment, and it pays off to keep a lookout for all the things, you need in order to prepare your ship for the sea. Small improvements for little money and sustainable recycling walk hand in hand. To give an old cheap boat an extended life by making it relevant and updating its equipment is basic sustainability. And you can reuse literally everything, you use on a boat except for sheets, mooring lines and batteries. And it can be quite fun too, if you can acquire an old VHF-radio or an echosounder as working retro gadgets. Refurbishing and preserving an old boat and reusing redundant equipment from others is pure sustainability. Far less harmful on the environment than scrapping both boat and electronic equipment.

11. SAILS

The sails are some of the most important items onboard. Here are some thoughts on spending money on sails. When I bought my 22 ft. Marsvin (a double ender by Danish designer Peter Bruun), a brand new high aspect jib from North Sails and a sorry old rag of a jib were part of the wardrobe. I decided to retire the old rag and start using the new sail. How happy I was for that decision. All boats sail better with a new flat foresail. Less heel and improved windward performance is the major difference. On the other hand a solid old mainsail is all you need for cruising. Our present mainsail has more than 15 seasons in its wake so far. The foresail is absolutely essential for comfort, speed and windward performance.

So if you wish to spend money on the luxury of a new sail and only can afford one, buy a jib. It's like having a new boat. It sails better and is far easier to handle. If you choose a boat type with many boats built, you can be fortunate enough to get cheap good used sails. In the Nordic Folkboat class for instance, relatively new sails are obtainable, because people who race their yachts, change them after one or two seasons. If you choose a rare boat, then that is virtually impossible. When we cleared the stock of old but still good sails, they sold for 100-200 € or 10-15% of the price of new ones. There is no need to collect a stock of old sails. Get rid of them and let others enjoy a better sail.

Sails can be repaired and have their stiching mended, even if the sails are torn. And it often pays. Find a local sailmaker with a good reputation for mending and repairing at reasonable costs.

On our first sailboat - a Hurley 20 from 1969 - we had a complete set of sails from 1969, and they still worked alright. Of course we didn't beat particularly high to windward with old hollow sails on a boat with bilge keels, but we didn't have anything to compare them with, and when I read my log from that time, there is not one mentioning of it. But with the knowledge I have today, I would have recommended myself to put money aside for a new jib.

For cruising a small boat, I would recommend the following sail configuration: Mainsail + a jib + a spinnaker (or a genoa for the less experienced crew). Then you still have stowage space for kit bags and provisions and your crew. You probably don't need more than the three sail configuration and won't be missing a midsized genoa nor the storm jib for that matter. The spinnaker is a luxury item to bring on a cruise, because of the stowage space it occupies, but the reward is gained momentum and fun pleasant sailing on days, where a warm light downwind is all you have. You will be rid of the temptation to start the engine. Sailboats almost always sail better under sail.

When cruising and moored in a foreign port, we used to roll up our jib and tie it to the searail, so as not to take up valuable living space in the confined quarters down below.

12. ENGINE

If minimalism is a demand, then I would suggest a smaller boat equipped with an outboard engine over an inboard.

The outboard engine is relatively simple, and a professional servicing at the time of purchase and a yearly DIY greasing and cleaning will keep you going for several years. And you will have an engine, that will not fail you when running idle or put in reverse, running for hours on end all day long if needed. Two-stroke engines are now discontinued, but there are a lot of them out there, and they are more reliable and less sensitive. On the other hand, they are a bit noisier and oil should be added meticulously to petrol in the right mix, when bunkering fuel for your cruise. Evinrude has in recent years developed a new environmentally friendly two-stroke engine with separate oil compartment and long servicing intervals.

It is far more pleasant to run a four-stroke engine, as it is quiet but also more expensive and requires more servicing for operational trustworthiness. Make sure, that your engine is always well kept and in working order. In this way you will remove much of the stress and apprehension from your outings.

Some of the boats in this book come with an inboard, but they are far more common in the 26-28 ft. class. It is the single most expensive investment in a boat and the greatest cause for uncertainty when buying an old boat. On top of that you should expect a cost for annual servicing in the amount of 250-400 €, unless you are able to change the impeller for the water pump, oil filter and engine oil yourself. Spare parts like exhaust elbows (the last part of the manifold, where it connects with the exhaust) and rubber membranes for S-drives must be changed at certain intervals and incur more fixed costs. Finally the engines break down, and they are far more expensive to repair than outboards. That needs to be considered in choosing one boat over the other. The inboard engine however, is also a huge convenience, and there is nothing better than turning the ignition key and drive the gear and throttle handle forward. Maneuvering your boat in marinas is also less complicated with an inboard.

An installation of a new inboard diesel engine will easily cost in excess of 13,000 €, and in comparison you will get a fine new outboard engine for 1,100 to 2,000 €. An old inboard engine poses a far bigger investment risk than an old outboard.

"One should not sail far but sail good"
- Peer Bruun

A couple of pocket cruisers at a jetty in Svendborg Sound

13. UNDERWAY, IN PORT AND AT ANCHOR

When you sail from your home port to a foreign destination, it is a virtue to familiarise yourself with the local conditions, where you sail, as well as the sailing conditions along your route: Shoals to be aware of passing at a safe distance, beacons, notable landmarks for your navigation, and not the least the weather conditions of the day. You can find everything on the net or from several excellent apps for smartphones, but you must not make yourself dependent on mobile coverage underway. Check it before departure. It is called passage planning. Calculate the total distance in nautical miles and divide it by your estimated average sailing speed taking the wind conditions into consideration. Then you have the estimated hours spent sailing from A to B. Add one or two hours depending on the length of your passage leg to be on the safe side. Write down the most important waypoints on a paper pad, so that you can check your passage plan underway.

"The sails determine the course - not the wind"
- Johann Wolfgang von Goethe

Navigation and backup systems

I assume, that you will wish to use a navigation app on your smartphone or tablet with digital seacharts. Remember, that all electronics may fail or run out of power. Navigation is a serious discipline, one should never take lightly. Keep one or more backup systems, of which paper charts make up one of them. On my very first three day cruise leaving the homely sheltered bay in my first boat, my Garmin GPS broke down on the morning of going back, and my initial reaction was panic and fear: Help! I am lost! Then I reminded myself, that I had learned to navigate with a chart and a compass, and of course I would be able to get my bearings straight and find the way home for my son and I. And we did. I have given Garmin many a thankful thought for the valuable lesson learned. I am a skipper. I am a competent navigator, and that's what I do - even when the assistive technology fails.

In a small boat it is fully adequate to have paper charts and a simple course ruler and binoculars with built in bearing compass. I sailed throughout the entire season of 2019 in this way. Doing without the GPS plotter gives you a

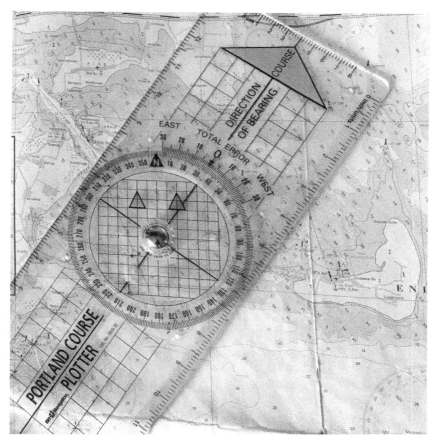

Portland Course Plotter is a solid navigational ruler, a potential replacement for the parallel ruler and the triangle ruler. It takes 30 seconds to put a bearing into the map and even shorter to lay a course.

newfelt freedom and a different sense of presence in the sailing: You simply
have to be more aware and attentive, when the plotter isn't available.

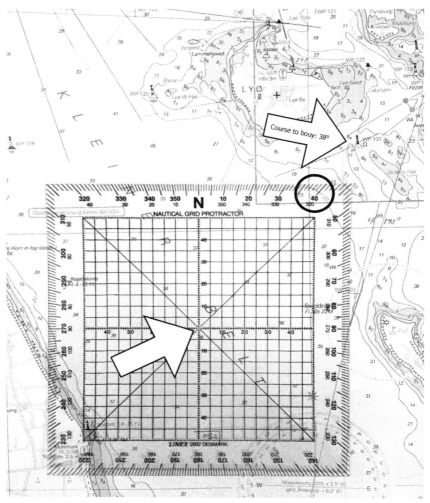

Linex 2802 is a simple and easy course plotter. It is placed with the known position in the middle -
north up. The course is read in the direction you wish to sail, read along the edge.

On the other hand it could be a really good investment to purchase a small compact plotter with a fine bright monitor, giving you free hands for the helm and sheets, if you sail alone much of the time. But I would still recommend new yacht size paper charts on the side. You orientate yourself much better on a paper chart than a small monitor. They come with a practical plastic folder, so that they can be left on the cockpit seat in all kinds of weather.

"Set your course by the stars,
not by the lights of every passing ship"
- Omar N. Bradley

In the previous two pictures you will see two course rulers, which I have been using. The Linex plotter is super simple, when you know where you are and need to know the bearing to the next waypoint. The dot in the middle is placed on the known position (north up), and you put your finger in the direction, you wish to sail and read the bearing of the compass course in the edge of the ruler. However, it is not suitable for putting a compass bearing into the chart, which is far easier using a traditional triangle ruler and a straight ruler.

I have used a Portland Course plotter during the 2019 season, and the only disadvantage of it is, that it's somewhat big for the yacht size charts, but you learn to accept it. On the other hand it is so fast and precise in plotting your course or putting a compass bearing into the chart. The guiding principle navigating in a small boat and even more so as a single hand sailor is speed and simplicity. During the seconds when the sails are flapping and the boat is getting off course, you must be able to get your bearings and get back to the helm and pull in the sheets again. Sailing with a chart and a compass is fun and enriches the sailing experience with an improved presence.

What is your plan for approach?

When preparing for landfall and approach of a harbour, involve your crew in your plan: Where do we expect to look for a vacant berth? What does the harbour look like, when we get in behind the breakwater? A yacht harbour guide is good to include in your ship's library, and you could make do with a second hand copy. Try to keep your mooring lines tied to the clamps and ready before approaching, fenders tied to the sea railing and lying ready on deck. I prefer to let the boat go into the wind just outside the harbour, taking down the sails and making them fast with the engine idling. If I am alone, I put it into reverse with low revolutions. The boat will keep still with the stern to the wind, while I move about on deck.

If you bring a crew, tell them, where you would want them to be while entering port and ask them to sit down, so that you will be able to concentrate and get an overview. The foredeck crew can sit on the coachroof near you, so you can talk in the process without shouting. When you moor in a pile berth, it is important to get a mooring line on the windward pile (where the wind comes from).

Boats already moored to starboard and port are responsible for fendering off properly. If you decide to keep your fenders hanging over the side, only do it close to the stem, so you won't risk getting stuck on the piles when coming in.

Your crew should keep a fender ready to put between your boat and the leeward boat. Far too many fumble and tumble and react hectic in the situation. But it doesn't have to be stressful. You being the skipper at the helm will slow down the boat either with the engine or the aft mooring lines, and your crew should call the distance "2 metres!" "1 metre!" and "STOP!" in time before you hit the jetty.

If you sail a boat in the range from 16-28 ft., you will always find a berth or a place to moor in any harbour. It is not the length but the beam, that will narrow down the possibilities. With a beam of more than 3 metres it will get more difficult. If you don't find a berth straight away, you should buy yourself time to get an overview by mooring temporarily at a pile with the stem to windward, while you make out a new plan of action. If you find yourself in a tight spot and a sudden squal with little room for maneuvering, you could try to put your engine in reverse and move ever so slowly astern. Like I described before, the boat will come to an almost stand still with the stern to the wind and give you the opportunity to await a more favourable moment to go ahead, give it throttle and come about.

Mooring charges are often quite expensive from a pocket cruising money perspective, though you are almost lynched for saying that in social sailing media. In Denmark we have a few free ports, who have agreed among themselves to give their boat owners favourable low prices on spending 1-3 nights in their marinas.

Lying at anchor however, is free, just like the bouys placed by the Danish Sailing Association and Danish Cruising Association. It does require, that you are a member of one of these associations though, if you use them. But a good anchor in the right weight class is a must for you with a small boat. Apart from being an essential safety equipment it is also a pleasure to drop anchor in a fine sheltered place in the lee of land. The quiet tranquillity is indescribable. Plough anchors, Bruce anchors and Danforth anchors are the types typically mentioned as the best under most conditions. The Rocna anchor is quite expensive but indisputably a great anchor. Similar but cheaper ones, which probaby also work fine are readily available. You should have a proper length of anchor chain and at least 30 metres of anchor rope.

"If one does not know to which port one is sailing,
no wind is favorable."
- Seneca

14. SELECTED EXAMPLES OF SMALL CRUISING BOATS AND EXPERIENCES

The following selection of sailboats are predominantly boats, found in Danish harbours and waters, partly represented as well in northern Germany and western and southern Sweden. As the Danish sailing scene in the 1960's and 1970's was also greatly influenced by the GRP building boom in Britain, a lot of British sailors will no doubt recognise many of the British golden age GRP sailboats.

Both Britain and Germany differ somewhat compared to the present Danish sailing scene with ever bigger boats, as the two countries are also characterised by a counter tendency towards pocket cruisers. Quite a few boat designers and boat yards in Britain build modern traditional looking craft in small numbers, and in Germany a handful of designers and yards design and build daysailers and small craft for rivers and lakes.

The pool of resources among the many thousands of vintage GRP pocket cruisers afloat or resting ashore comprise a lucrative base for a generation of recycled, refurbished and upcycled sailboats with potential for a renewed revalued life second time around. Coming full circle in the hands of new generations of enthusiastic micro adventurers. Restored or reinvented and reinterpreted to fullfil and satisfy a present day understanding of the need to go to sea.

Alacrity 19

LOA (Length overall) 5.64 m, Beam 2.11 m, Draft 0.55 m, 680 kg, 14 m² sail area. Designed in 1960 by Peter Stevenson and built by Hurley Marine for Russel Marine. Like many of small craft from the British golden age of GRP in the 60's, the Alacrity looks rather old fashioned, but it adds considerably to it's present classical charm. It regularly turns up in used boat portals, indicating quite a few circulating boats around. See also her sistership, Vivacity 20.

Albin Accent 26

LOA 8.05 m, Beam 2.77 m, Draft 1.54 m, 2,300 kg, 34 m² sail area. Designed by Peter Norlin in 1974. 650 boats were built.

Martin Sørensen regarding his first boat an Accent 26: "We looked at bigger boats, but it had to be affordable and easy to handle. That put some limitiations to the decision, but on the other hand you get loads of "hygge" (snug, cosy), which you might not find in bigger boats. Accent 26 is a classic 70's boat with its toprig and giant genoa. Since this particular boat has a rather unusual installation of the engine in the foreship, it offers quite roomy quarter berths and a total of four permanent berths two in the forepeak + two aft and a settee berth in the cabin, if the table is lowered. The boat has a wide beam and fine sailing characteristics. With its narrow waterline and beamy hul it is tender (low initial stability) and at first it heels over and then begins to quickly right itself, as it picks up speed. It is lively and sporty but does not in any way feel unsafe - not even in a gale force wind. It just takes a little getting used to. We are facing the Baltic Sea in Fakse Ladeplads - also known as the "Biscay" of Denmark, and it does just fine in this environment. It reacts instantly to the helm and to changes in trim. We are old scouts and sail with our two children, so even if the boat has lots of spacious comfort, we are far from using all, it has to offer. We had a 110% genoa tailored for the boat, which has eased the handling in windward conditions with only a modest speed loss in lighter airs."

Albin Express

LOA 7.7 m, Beam 2.49 m, Draft 1.45 m, 1,800 kg, 32,5 m^2 sail area. Designed by Peter Norlin in 1979. More than 1,100 boats were built. The Express is lively and sporty and therefore won widespread acclaim as a racing yacht, but actually it is a very well performing family cruiser with somewhat simpler comfort. The class is still very active on the racing scene and also has an active class organisation in Denmark, Sweden and Germany and gathers participants enough for a northern European Championship.

The Albin Express Explorer during the Danish Championship of 2019. Photo: Peter Brøgger

Albin Viggen

LOA 7.10 m, Beam 2.24 m, Draft 1.0 m, 1,400 kg, 30 m² sail area. Viggen was designed by Per Brohäll, who also designed the larger Albin Vega. By the way, the name is Swedish for "tufted duck." Viggen was first built as the Karlskrona Viggen from 1971 and later as the Albin Viggen, and more than 1,650 were built over the years from 1971 to 1978.

Bertram's first boat "Mona" named after a popular song by Søren Kragh Jakobsens "Kender du det," an idea originated by Bertram's 10 year old younger brother.

When Bertram was 17 years old, he bought an Albin Viggen from 1973 for 1,200 € from an old man, who was giving up on sailing. "And so my happiness was made. I literally fixed it with duck tape and simplified as much as possible. A top lantern, a lamp below and a big battery with power for weeks. The simpler the cheaper! I had her for barely 18 months, until I had to sell her for money reasons. I spent a lot of money on her, but one should regard it as money put into experiences and not into the boat."

"I bought her before Easter of 2017, while I attended general upper secondary school and was living aboard the boat in Kastrup in Øresound (the Sound). I biked nine kilometers to school every morning and only had a single burner alcohol stove and a sink, which also served as the companionway step." Bertram explains the interior layout: "It is not really very well thought out - it has a classic furnishing with a sofa on either side and a triangle forepeak berth. The berths are so low, that one sits with the knees right under the chin. The cabin table also serves as a cockpit table but is way too high for sitting comfortably. I took away the mattress from the port berth and mounted a tabletop aligned with the stove and sitting on a milkbox, I could do my homework. In the quarter berth I stacked up boxes for my stuff and a shoe shelf. I slept in the bow on one side with a laundry basket on the other. During winter I placed isolating mattresses on deck with wooden boards on top of them. The boat had an oil heating stove, which was extremely efficient, but I was in for some bad luck: One night the exhaust tube fell off and filled the entire cabin with smoke. I was woken by a smoke alarm and though paralysed managed to call my mother. Thanks to her help I survived and escaped the ordeal with a slight carbon monoxide poisoning and a few days in hospital. My friends gave me an oil-filled electrical radiator for Christmas as a replacement for the defective heater."

"During the summer of 2017 I sailed with a couple of mates to Horsens on the east cost of Jutland and continued alone round Denmark for seven weeks. The boat was fitted with a furling genoa and an old mainsail without reefs. It was the best summer, I ever had. I just loved its sailing characteristics, though it didn't match the many far more modern boats. But that didn't take away the joy of sailing it. I rigged a couple of lines to steer it from below in foul weather. I didn't have proper anchoring gear, so I just moored at the mooring buoys laid out by the Sailing Association and at one time even a green marker buoy. I took it all very lightly. My parents wanted me to save up

900 €, if I were supposed to sail away for a week. The money lasted for seven weeks of sailing, and I still had 500 € when I returned home. It even took me by surprise, that I had not spent more money. I was a little teenage-naive at the time, thinking back on the decisions I made. I am happy, it all went so well." Among other things, Bertram managed a situation with a broken aft stay in bad weather throwing himself at the topping lift with his modest body weight and swing the boat round into the wind. After a quick repair, he was off again soon after.

Meanwhile, 20 year old Bertram did a formal maritime training on the training ship Georg Stage and has once again set foot on his own deck. He bought an old Shipman 28 "in a half critical condition but really good looking. Despite a low purchasing price, the totals sum up to 11,000 €, but now it gradually presents itself in a near mint condition after some three months of intensive labour. My boat needs to be small enough to enter port under sail, if I have to. I will travel far with my Shipman 28. Northwest Africa for example." Bertram insisted on mentioning his Shipman 28, even though it's actually too big to fit the scope of this book. He earned it though with his wonderful story. Bertrams new boat was named after his mother Astrid.

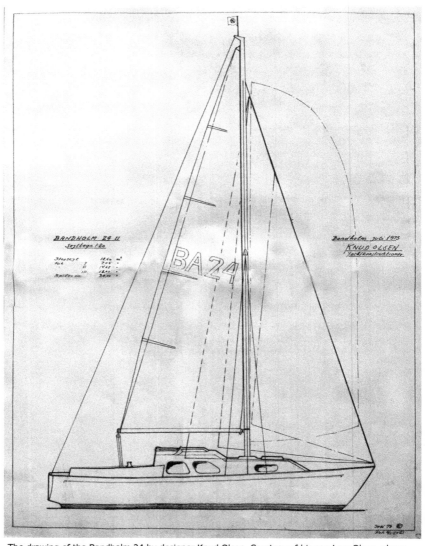

The drawing of the Bandholm 24 by designer Knud Olsen. Courtesy of his son Lars Olsen, also a naval architect and designer of the well known L23.

A genuine classic the Bandholm 24. Photo: André Christensen

Bandholm 24

LOA 7.2 m, Beam 2.3 m, Draft 1.3 m, 2,200 kg, 23 m² sail area.

Designed by Knud Olsen in 1971. The classic harmonious Bandholm 24 always had a reputation of living up to the yard's motto "swift, safe and solid." BA24 is truly a fine sailing boat, which earned the reputation of being a fast boat and still a treasured sailboat for cruising. It is the epitome of a classic pocket cruising yacht. More than 300 boats were built.

André Christensen bought his Bandholm 24 five years ago from an elderly gentleman giving up sailing. The boat's name was Sirius, and André came straight from his service at Daneborg Arctic Station in his polar gear with the badge of the Sirius Patrol on his jacket. So he was instantly hooked: "Bandholm 24 is actually both a good and a bad sailboat. She is a tough boat, that will take any gale force wind. But she also needs a fairly strong wind and has a plesant moving characteristic in a swell. In less than 10 knots of wind, it doesn't move at all. Otherwise, you will need a spinnaker or gennaker for it. It's a heavy displacement boat with 50% keel weight, and I have tried to sail her in a 30 knot NE gale in the bay of Køge. We were tossed about, but the boat on the whole made her way through it perfectly well and remained almost dry."

At 3,500 € it's an amazing sailboat to start your family sailing career. My wife isn't used to sailing, and we have two small children. The boat is by far the most stable I have sailed." André repaired the balsa layer in the coachroof and made a new mast support, typical observation points on 40-50 year old sailboats. Bandholm 24 was one of the first 24 ft. boats with a sea toilet onboard in the front cabin. "I changed the interior, so that all the cabin can become one big berth. It makes it a stable and safe boat, when you are sailing with an infant and a girl of four. When you are moored to a jetty, people stop by for a chat and a closer look, because it's a Bandholm. It's a heavy boat to dance with during harbour maneuvres, but when conditions freshen up at sea, it is incredibly safe with a strong directional stability and just takes off. I plan trips ahead from home based on an average speed of 3,5

André and his family onboard their Bandholm 24

knots. It is quite accurate in my experience. In a fresh breeze it sails approximately 5-7 knots."

"Down below stowage space is rather limited. At best it fits a weekend bag. The pantry table is below the companionway. The boat has a deep keelson because of the long keel and shallow draft, which means, that we can sail almost everywhere we like. This year we've sailed some 600 nautical miles. It really comes down to the possibility to go sailing. The boat has room for five people. We can cook hot and cold food. The boat is equipped with an old fashioned icebox and running water, and you can wash your hands. It is catharsis (Greek) =   An utter purification to sail. We like to anchor and love waking up in places like the Bøgestrøm fairlead, the Sound or the Southern Funen Archipelago."

Carina 20

LOA 5.96 m, 2.11 m, Draft 0.90 m, 850 kg, 18.6 m2. Sitting headroom 1.25 m. Designed by Günther Thomat in 1962. Built in both Germany and later in Poland in significant numbers.

The Carina 20 was originally a plywood design but was transformed later to a GRP design and is quite well known in both its native Germany as in Denmark. Its lines are quite accomplished for its size, and the sailing performance is good. Carina also had two bigger sisters, the 23 ft. Marina and the 26 ft. Sabrina. All built by Marina Werft GmbH. Though a modest little craft, a young Hungarian Aron Meder circumnavigated the globe in a Carina in 2009. A heroic achievement.

Throughout his life, Bent Flemming Nielsen wanted to sail but was never able to afford it. Now in his retirement, he was given the opportunity to take over an old Carina 20 for 75 € and since July 2019 he has been working on a gradual restoration. The boat stood on land with water inside, and a refurbishment of the interior is needed, before it once again regains its past power and glory.

During autumn he managed to retrieve various bits and pieces of rigging and sails from different addresses in Jutland and making the boat ready to sail. After some years of assisting in sailing for the disabled and being a sailing instructor, he is well prepared to become captain of his own vessel now.

The Carina was actually supposed to be a Rügen sailing dinghy, but as it turned out, sailing dinghies are far more expensive than small keelboats. So that is obviously how things are supposed to be then. Bent managed a few sailing trips in autumn to test the sailing performance and with the aid of additional water ballast also managed to make the boat motor acceptable. The boat, which is named Pusling, rode off the winter gales in water and is now due for the next step of the refit and above all, what Bent has dreamed about for so long.

'Pusling' the Carina 20 of Bent Flemming Nielsen. Private photo by the owner

The Drabant 22 Smølf II owned by Henrik Jæger. Photo: Knud Erik Schulz.

Drabant 22

LOA 6.64 m. Beam 2.1 m. Draft 1.1 m. 990 kg. 25 m^2 sail area. Designed by Gert Gerlach in 1968. 225 boats were built. The Drabant 22 in my opinion is a true classic Danish pocket cruiser with its simplistic beautiful lines.

Henrik Jæger: "I'm 54 years old and started my sailing career in a Snipe dinghy but bought my Drabant 22 Smølf five years ago. I intended it to offer shelter and comfort at a low cost. I refitted the boat quite a lot: New sliding hatch, painted deck coachroof and cockpit, and in part the sandwich construction in the coachroof was repaired and renewed. As well as lots of little updates within reason. I like to use my hands. It wasn't until this year, that I bought a new furling headsail. Otherwise I might as well buy second hand gear. I have only been away on a singlehanded cruise on one occasion. However, I take part in the yach races in Nappedam, where I come in last every time. But it is so enjoyable and not very competitive. The boat is incredibly easy to sail, so it's always a pleasure sailing it alone. Everything is within reach."

Ole Faurschou tells the tale of his Drabant Marie D185: "I find the Drabant harmonious in both appearance and behaviour. She's lively and fun. And the boat is so tiny, that it moves, when you walk across it, and you have to sit properly in it. You are rewarded with good speed and a sensible way of moving through the water. It is fast, and often you can outsail the slightly bigger boats. It has really good windward performance and sails well with a big genoa from light airs to a fair breeze of 12-16 knots of wind."

"The boat is moored in Humlum in the Limfjord. One of the longer passages, I have made, went to Sørlandet Lyngør in Norway via Nissum Bredning and Hanstholm in the Northsea. I sailed the 80 nautical miles to Grimstad with an average of 5.5 knots. The skerries are situated in the lee of the west winds, and everywhere it is very green and beautiful."

The Drabant 22 Marie D185

"The children grew up in that boat. We have been sailing two adults and two small children for several days at a time. It is quite small, and there isn't much room. You have to take turns doing different things or wait for the other crew member to brush her teeth etc. We went on a trip to Livø this summer with two nights out and now four adults. It did work out. One quarter berth was reserved for luggage, so one of us had to sleep on the cabin floor. Having had that experience, I see no reason to buy a bigger boat. I have often sailed with friends and also singlehanded in the Drabant. It also has the advantage of closeness with the water. You instantly sense, if the trim is bad. There are also things that are easier, when you own a small boat. A couple of years ago we rented a large ketch in Greece, because we could afford it thanks to our modest boat budget."

Drabant 24

LOA 7.47 m, Beam 2.53 m, Draft 1.53 m, 2,120 kg, 32,6 m² sail area. Designed by Gert Gerlach in 1972. 165 boats have been built. It is a popular boat, that sails really well. It was an instant hit and today a very affordable boat to purchase.

Duet 25

LOA 7.62 m, Beam 2.56 m, Draft 1.4 m, 25 m² sail area. 1.633 kg. Designed by architect Vagn Møller in 1972 and built from 1974 by Th. Lind of Middelfart, a renowned builder of Folkboats. Duet 25 is a very accomplished attempt to modernise the Nordic Folkboat. The Duet has a self bailing cockpit, lower weight and a more spacious accomodation with an independent design language, while being true to its inspirational heritage. Probably one of the most beautiful yachts in the 24-25 ft. class.

The Duet 25 "Line"
Photo: Udo Nocera

A total of 56 boats were built. The Duet 25 is known for its convincing sailing characteristics. It is light and lively but an absolutely safe boat to sail. Udo Nocera sails his Duet 25 Line on Lake Möhnesee near Dortmund in Germany. The lake is dammed as a water reservoir for the Ruhr and Rhine rivers. Therefore the water level can change dramatically, when there is a need to flood the rivers more. You can always navigate the lake, but it can be a tight spot to access the slip and crane for launch and recovery.

Udo, a trained craftsman but an absolute beginner as a sailor and skipper, bought his Duet 25 in September 2018 and managed a brief debut on the water before hauling out. He then undertook a comprehensive refit with excellent advice from the experienced boat builders Sven Walther and Ralf Peine. Instead of polishing the worn old gelcoat he was advised to paint the boat. After demounting all fittings, it was sanded completely on the outside and painted by a car painter. The deck was laid with imitated teak, and the fine wooden mast was completely sanded down and varnished eight times with a two-component varnish and four layers of one-component varnish. Finally, the windows were replaced. The result is very accomplished indeed, though the refurbishment continues this winter. "But I also wanted to manage to sail the boat this season." He says. "Since we sail on Möhnesee and have to be able to pass under low bridges, we decided to install an electrical winch in the stem, thus enabling the lowering of the mast with the sails on it and pass bridges with only 3.5 metres of headroom."

"She sails remarkeably well for such an old boat, even compared to more modern boats with racier lines, that are supposed to be superior to the Duet. The strength of the Duet is clearly on windward courses and when tacking. It beats so high to windward, that you sometimes think it can actually sail against the wind, which of course it cannot. On the other hand, it doesn't sail particularly fast off the wind, which may be due to the displacement of some 2,200 kg. On the other hand it is very comfortable with its calm movements even in a strong wind, and I would describe it as more calm than sporty. It only heels slightly and is generally quite stiff and stable. It sails both better

and closer to windward, which gives it a good VMG - velocity made good - or speed to windward." Udo reckons, that its good speed when beating is a result of it being fresh painted and extremely smooth in the underwater hull and possibly its characteristic long clinker lines in the hull. Udo's more experienced sailor friend was equally surprised and enthusiastic over the sailing characteristics of the yacht. All the running rigging was exchanged with grey/olive recycled ropes made from old PET bottles by Toplicht in Hamburg and contribute to give the boat a very classic look along with the rubbing rail and wooden mast.

"We have very limited cruising experience so far with our boat, but the previous owners sailed her out of Marina Wendtorf off Kiel to the southern

Funen Archipelago almost every weekend come rain or rough waters. But it is so lovey for us, that she is so easily trailed. Möhnesee with its 5 kilometers is a great back yard for us to practice and learn."

Flemming Palm, an experienced sailor from Kerteminde had a Duet 25 for many years and offers the following testimony: "It easily earns its yardstick on Round Funen and other races. We always ended on top. Round Funen typically featured 10-12 Duets. As a cruising yacht and family boat you distinctly sense, that it is slightly bigger than the Folkboat. Well done Th. Lind! And it even offers a spinnaker. The class died, when the Duet sailors became too old for racing. The value of yachts is halved, when there is no longer a racing scene in the class. Cruising sailors are totally depending on the racing scene being intact. For that reason alone, the Duet is very affordable today."

In 2020 I undertook it to form a boat guild with a handful of fellow old salties to buy a Duet 25, which we offer for our members as a platform for fellowship, companionship and friendship across the usual segregation of gender and age. It is for both men and women, girls and boys from 13 and beyond who wish enjoy experiences in nature and life at sea - in a community with others to pass on your experience or learn the art of seamanship.

It is a community still in the making, but we have had very good response so far and already put a few nautical miles in the wake of "Rasmine" - the boat was bought from new by the uncle of the seller and sailed with great affection - the boat was named after the beloved great grand mother of the first owner. The nephew and his wife named their middle daughter after the boat, which they too sailed for many years. Now the boat is the crankshaft of a community to produce a new breed of sailors, and the guild is already very fond of her.

Duet 25 "Rasmine" under sail with the happy boat guild and its cosy below quarters. The boat is very well cared for by its previous owners and a wonderful craft for the large Bay of Kerteminde and the Great Belt in the Baltic Sea dividing the island of Funen from Zealand to the east.

Edel 545

LOA 5.45 m, Beam 2.44 m, Draft 0.7 m, 550 kg, 15 m² sail area. Designed in 1974 by Maurice Edel. More than 2,500 boats were built. A successful design delivering wonderful sailing characteristics among the group of 18 footers with sporty bias and cruising capabilities for two. Also check out Edel 5, which is an identical model. Other models in the same series are definately worth considering. Check out Edel 6 and 660 with untraditional interior designs and solutions.

Edel 540. Foto: Ahunt, wikimedia.org (Creative Commons CCO 1.0)

Etap 22

LOA 6.6 m, Beam 2.4 m, Draft 1.25 m, 20 m^2 sail area. 1,400 kg. Designed by E. G. van de Stadt in 1974. 1,830 boats were built until 1984. Etap 22 received great reviews in the boat press for its sailing characteristics and untraditional solutions and is one of the very few unsinkable yachts on the market thanks to a foam core in the entire hull.

First 18

LOA 5.9 m, Beam 2.4 m, Draft 0.78 m, 17.5 m^2 sail area 600 kg. Designed by Jean Marie Finot in 1977. 1,065 boats were built between 1977 and 1983. The proportions of the tiny First 18 makes it both spacious and sporty thanks to its wide beam and flat bottom. With its shallow draft it can be dried out on its beam in tidal areas. The performance of the boat is quite good for its size. Furthermore, it is regarded as both comfortable and ergonomic. In my opinion it is also a beautiful and jaunty looking boat.

First 22

LOA 6.95 m, Beam 2.49 m, Draft 1.7 m, 26 m^2. sail area. 1,100 kg. Designed by Jean Marie Finot in 1978. 763 boats were built. A very successful design with fine lines where the kinship of First 18 is obvious.

Friendship 22

LOA 6.6 m, Beam 2.58 m, Draft 1.15/1.35 m, 25 m^2 sail area. 1,350 kg. Designed by Jac de Ridder in 1976.

Granada 24. Not the wedge shaped coach roof so typical of the 1970's. Photo: Lars Lindholm

Granada 24

LOA 7.14 m, Beam 2.52 m, Draft 1.25 m, 1,800 kg, 22.85 m^2 sail area. Standing headroom 1.72 m. Designed by Jørn Hansen in 1974. Some 432 Granada 24's were built.

Lars Lindholm of Fredericia on the East Jutland coast, tells the story of his Granada 24: "My boat was one of the very last built in 1979 with sail number 361 of 432. In a German review from 78, the Granada 24 is described as a "Raumwunder." My boat doesn't come with a lot of equipment and is rather simple equipped, but everything works. You almost need to upgrade to a Grinde size boat to experience spacious accomodation similar to the Granada. She offers up to five berths, provided two of the crew are little people. Her sailing performance is really good, but she is not especially fast. I sail her with a mainsail and a 30 m² genoa, and it is important to trim the traveller to avoid weather helm and being hard on the helm. One should actually just pay out on the mainsheet to regain the balance. This year I have been on a three week summer cruise with my girlfriend. We're both in our 50's. For five days a teenage son of 18 occupied the forepeak, and for the last week a daughter and her friend both in their 20's. Though it actually isn't very big, it's a wonderful cruising yacht. And it will take you anywhere and fit in any port." Under the name "Mekami" Lars' boat made a passage in the 80's to the Mediterranean and crossed the Bay of Biscay with her owners at the time - an elderly couple sailing off the Limfjord. "Personally, I mostly do short trips and preferably no longer than five-six hours at a time out of consideration for the crew. And I also participate in yacht racing as crew member onboard an X79."

"There is a marvellous community among people in small old boats. The fun of coming into port in a 24 ft. boat is, that people call out: "Over here, you can moor alongside us." The Granada was originally fitted out with an alcohol stove. And I managed to acquire the original Origo stove second hand. The toilet is a 39 year old RM69. Everything is solid and built with quality in mind. It's incredible, how you could build a boat in 1979, and everything is still in good working condition. There hasn't been any osmosis yet, and it is epoxy primed in the underwater hull. You can still get all the spares for the original French Isomât-mast even after 40 years. Both rudder and rudderstock are built in stainless steel, which makes it difficult to paint. You need to make the surface rough first with a steelbrush, before you can paint it. It is strongly built with a skeg in front for directional stability."

"Since the boat's draft is only 1.25 metres, you can almost sail her onto the beach, which happened to me this year on the island Lyø in the Southern Funen Archipelago. I wasn't paying attention and failed to reverse the outboard and very slowly sailed right onto the beach. A bathing holidaymaker waded out to my aid and gently pushed the boat back afloat. The shallow draft also makes it possible to cut corners and taking the easy route when approaching the island Endelave (off the east coast of Jutland), and generally many things are easier with a shallow draft. Near Trelde Næs - the southern point of the Vejle fjord - an enormous reef stretches out to sea. I sneak across the reef ever so carefully under engine. If one follows the draft curvature, it is navigable at a distance of approximately 50 metres from the coast."

Hallberg-Rassy Misil II

LOA 7.34 m, Beam 2.31 m, Draft 1.2 m, 28 m^2 sail area. 1,860 kg. Designed by Olle Enderlein in 1972. 596 boats were built. Misil II is a semi longkeeled masthead sloop. Misil displays fine lines and is an excellent example of the many successful designs by Olle Enderlein.

Misil II is known to be a fine allround sailboat. With its semi longkeel it is not particularly fast but does catch up with its waterline length. It is extremely safe, stable and well balanced. The sort of boat that behaves like a big boat but with the advantages of the smaller boat. The boat's sailing performance is excellent including courses to windward in strong wind and in a swell, where it rarely is stopped by a choppy sea. In that respect it resembles the qualities of among others the International Folkboat, Nordic Folkboat and Hurley 22.

One will always find a corner in any port with room for a 24 footer, and even the secluded smallboat ports for boats with shallow draft become accessible in the Misil II with its draft of 1.2 metres, which places it among the smallest of yachts - without being one - and in good company too.

Misil II is renowned for its build quality, and it is truly part of the Hallberg-Rassy pedigree. The boatyard actually has a handful of smaller sailboats on its conscience and not only the bigger and pricier ones, for which they are known nowadays. The cabin berths are fine and wide, and the living comfort is excellent in spite of lack of proper standing headroom.

Hurley 22

LOA 6.70 m, Beam 2.22 m, Draft 1.14 m, 1,768 kg. Sail area 22.30 m². The Hurley 22 is one of a handful of British boat types in the 22-26 ft. range, called the British folkboats with inspiration from the Nordic Folkboat. Designed by Ian L. Anderson in 1963. Hurley 22 has accomplished several remarkeable ocean passages and is extraordinarily seaworthy. More than 1,200 H22's have been built.

The first boat Bjarne Jensen owned was a Hurley 22, and it just sailed fantastically. He explains. It was much more of a sailboat than the Maxi 68, he replaced it with. "It was probably due to the triradial genoa and a new mainsail, that I bought from Elvström and spent a great deal of money on. It performed really well to windward. The genoa worked so well, even when reefed. I spent some long vacations in that boat, and I simply loved it. It was the boat for me. It sure was incredibly impractical in the interior layout, but as I sailed alone, it didn't matter. I sailed her to the western Swedish skerries for 6 weeks and got as far as Orust. I fell so much in love with the place, that I didn't get any further. The following year I sailed her to Visby on Gotland in the Baltic Sea. Underway, I sailed via Karlskrona and picked up a mate. All summer it was blowing gale force winds. We split the harbour dues, but all of a sudden the mate stated, he could not afford to sail on. But it was probably the rough weather and a disagreement whether or not to proceed to Fårö. In any case, the mate went ashore, and I sailed on to Fårö."

"Then I had a call from another mate, who asked if I could pick him up at the island Bornholm and sail him to Poland, as he had met a woman and wanted to travel with her to the Ukraine. Then our passports were stolen, and we were forced to go by train to Gdansk and acquire new passports, before being allowed to leave Poland again. From there we sailed on to Rügen in Germany and enjoyed ourselves for a couple of days before heading back to Sønderborg in the south of Jutland. Sailwise it was the best trip ever."

Hurley 22. Pictures and drawings from the Hurley Marines marketing courtesy of Hurley Owners Association

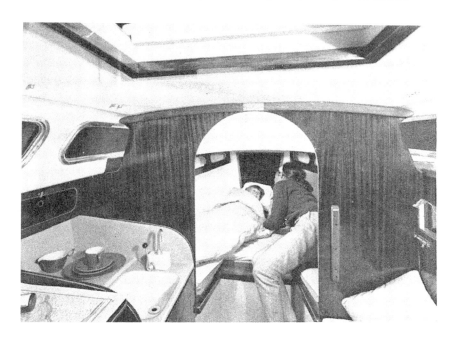

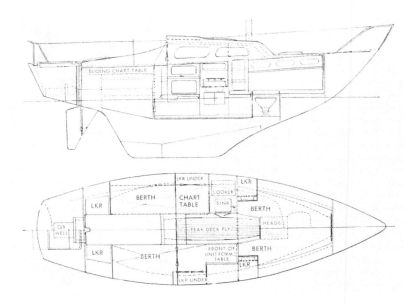

Hurley 22 is one many British yachts of the 1960's inspired by the Nordic Folkboat

The Hurley 22 is built with an outboard well for a long legged outboard engine. Nowadays modern british small craft are always built with an outboard well, and the system has now been improved with means of closing the hole, when the outboard is tilted or lifted out of the water while sailing.

The Hurley 22 owners offer quite different opinions as to the useability of the well. On one hand it is practical and gives a pleasant sailing in a choppy sea while going forward. On the other hand it is rather hopeless in astern with the propeller sitting behind the rudder, which is far from ideal. It is more likely a temperamental issue, but surely a plus not having to lean over the stern to handle it. And also that the prop doesn't come out of the water in a swell like most other boats with outboards.

LÄNGD ÖVER ALLT   7,85 MTR
BREDD   2,25   "
DEPLACEMENT   2,15 TON
SEGELAREA   26 KVM

INTERNATIONELLA FOLKBÅTEN
(THE INTERNATIONAL FOLKBOAT)
SKALA 1:25
GÖTEBORG 15-9-66
TORD SUNDÉN

RITN. NR. 1237

1237

91

International Folkboat - Marieholm IF

LOA 7.87 m, Beam 2.2 m, Draft 1.21 m, 2,150 kg. 31 m^2 sail area.

The IF boat was designed by Tord Sundén in 1966. It's a fantastic sailboat, that people get stuck in year after year instead of moving on to bigger class boats. It sails really well and is a genuine cruising boat. More than 3,500 boats were built, and they are available in the brokerage market for really reasonable prices. Lately production of the IF boat was resumed under the name of Seacamper IF in Germany at an introductory price of 47,000 €, which is quite affordable for a solid sailing classic small family boat. See chapter 14 for pictures of the new generation IF.

Gry Maria Kjaer Sørensen took over her father's IF boat Nausikaa: "This year we went on a sailing vacation for the first time with the children, Bille at two years and Cleo at seven, in the IF with which I have been sailing since I was six years old, whern my father bought it with a friend. Before leaving, I had plenty of advice from the Facebook group "Tursejlads og Sejlsport" ("Cruising and Sailing") about many things like making new matresses and a lot of other things. Parenting small children in their defiance age is bloody hard work - but it was worth everything. We returned home with quite marvellous memories, and the children learned lots of things. We only sailed along the coast in Danish waters for a couple of weeks, as we had decided to start nice and quiet with the children. It turned out to be a good strategy, as both children are totally hooked on sailing now.

"The urge to sail came from my father. He has always sailed. I remember the very first summer vacation, where we were underway for four weeks. Since then we sailed three-four weeks every year. We had no time to waste. We just took off on the S/Y "Nausikaa:" Me, my bigger sister, Mum and Dad. Later we brought a friend, and we three girls of 12-13 years occupied the forpeak for a great part of the cruise. We didn't even think once, that there wasn't room

enough. When we visited other children onboard their much bigger boats, we did notice, how much space they had, but it didn't matter to us. We cruised the Danish and Swedish waters including the skerries. When we became real teenagers, we took a few years off doing road trips in the US experiencing Grand Canyon and other cool places. But the happiness of the childhood years were stored in that boat. That boat contains emotions of happiness and freedom."

Danish hygge down below for Cleo, Bille and Niklas

Cleo is busy with the much wanted job of doing the dishes on the quayside

"I hardly remember any really bad weather during my childhood sailing vacations. Maybe I am romanticising my recollection, but I clearly remember the first time we experienced a thunder storm onboard, and my dad said: "Nothing can happen on a sailboat. The mast is like a lightning rod." So my sister and I just had a cosy relaxed time. Now I know, it's not entirely true, but I would probably tell my children the same."

"It was also fascinating to do the passage planning and knowing, we would be riding out a gale for a couple of days in port. It was kind of exciting to be pinned down. Now we had to find something else to do. So maybe we would sit and play cards onboard."

"We only sail with charts and a compass and don't have much money to put into it. We don't need a lot of gear and equipment. It actually felt quite cool, figuring it out. And I did learn to navigate. We don't even have a toilet onboard. And only a single burner electric stove. This year we only spent the nights in ports and not at anchor. As we don't have a fridge, we buy milk every morning and what else, we need and no more than that. The children think, that everything we do is really interesting. Like doing the dishes on the quayside, which is transformed into time alone with one of the children. They fought each other for getting to do the dishes throughout the holiday. At home we cannot make them do it."

"Cleo, our oldest was so afraid of being on a boat when she was younger, so it was important to make it a good experience. Now she is jumping around. It gives you a good feeling to see, and it shows, that you should never give up. You have to sail on the childrens' terms, so that you can keep doing it. We only sail a few hours a day, which sometimes turn into five-six hours. And it is not easy with a two year old boy, but for now the two of them are just looking forward to getting away on the boat again next summer. Sometimes we do think, how wonderful it would be with standing headroom. But it is also difficult to abandon such a ship, where you grew up. My father still has the possibility to sail with us, whenever he feels like it, and he knows, we look after the boat and tend to it. We wrote a little e-mail logbog diary for him every day on the trip. He and I both enjoyed it thoroughly."

"Sailing is such an adventure - even here in Denmark. Sometimes we just sail a few miles from Elsinore to Sletten. When we approach the port, my daughter Cleo asks: "Which country are we in now Mummy?"

"An ordinary pasta dish after an outing at sea can be quite a feast. As the skipper I can see, that I am quite the spontaneous type. And gosh what an enormeous responsibility I have."

"My husband Niklas isn't accustomed to sailing, so I cannot share it with him at present. And he needs to be in charge of the kids. We are not the sort of parents, who park the children in the cabin with an iPad. They can do that while at home."

Jaguar 22

LOA 6.55 m, Beam 2.34 m, Draft 1.06 m, 17.65 m² sail area. 1,190 kg. Designed in 1969 by Frank V. Butler and probably the sailboat to have been built in the highest number in the world with more than 16,000 under the name Catalina 22 in the US and Canada and Jaguar 22 in Britain as well as a number of other names. The boat is described as a family friendly trailer sailer with reliable sailing characteristics. For a generation the Jaguar 22 has defined the small family boat for sailors around the world. As a trailer sailer it is somewhat heavy and will require a fairly bigger car for towing.

Catalina 22 / Jaguar 22. Probably the most built sailboat worldwide.
Photo: Ahunt, Wikimedia (Creative Commons CCO 1.0)

Junker 22

LOA 6.5, m, Beam 1.98 m, Draft 0.9 m, 18.8 m² sail area. 1,470 kg. Designed by Arne Borghegn in 1971. In total 518 boats were built.

The paradox of the Junker is, that many sailors don't hold it in high regard, but it has proved its seaworthiness and sailing performance by circum navigating the globe. It is a traditional yacht with a longkeel and moderate rig. And its owners cherish and appreciate it. When I was 15, I strolled down the jetties of Kolding Marina and always paused and dreamed, if only I had such a Junker 22. It looked kind of cosy.

Junker 22. Photo: Kristoffer Jensen

Kristoffer Jensen: "I bought a Junker 22 from 1972 in January this year. It was in pretty bad shape. Parts of the interior had to be replaced and we gave it a complete makeover down below. We will continue outside next fall. We took it on outings from The Copenhagen South Port to Køge, Vallensbæk, Brøndby and Dragør - primarily on daytrips or with one or two nights spent aboard. I have been sailing for many years, but my girlfriend hasn't, so it was important to find a boat, which was easy to sail. It also means, that you quickly learn the important aspects of sailing a boat, and she has already picked up a lot of skills. We will sail her for a couple of years, to make sure my girlfriend really likes it, and we haven't spent much money on the boat yet."

"The Junker is a fantastic boat. It is really great that it only draws 90 cm. We can sail all the way on to the beach at maybe 1.2-1.3 metres and wade in. It works well for two people cruising. We sleep in the quarter berths aft. In the forepeak one has to throw in a little more optimism to fit in, and it is not that comfortable, unless you're really fond of one another. It was primarily designed for sitting in the cockpit, which offers a good length and lots of room. We have been daysailing with six adults onboard. We go out for sailing and the fresh air. We are however somewhat challenged on days of foul weather. A cockpit tent would be a good idea to consider. The standing headroom is 160-170 cm right by the sliding hatch, and you need to coordinate with each other, if you wish to switch places. The boom is placed high enough for not having to duck, and it is adjustable."

"It's a safe but slow sailboat not built for racing. It's windward performance isn't that great, but it sails far better with the wind abeam or when close reaching. It simply sits well in the water. The sails are the original vintage 1972, which also explains the windward performance. One cannot sheet in the old genoa enough to sail closer to the wind. But the cool thing about the mainsail is, that it is sheeted from a traveller. I played a bit with it, and it helped gain a bit better performance to windward. I have been happy with it, because I have an inexperienced girlfriend, who hasn't done much sailing. Otherwise I would have preferred a somewhat faster yacht. But for us, who are not going on long round Zealand trips, she is fine. You quickly sense, if there is a response from changes to the trim. The boat only weighs 1,400 kg, and even the slightest puff of air transforms into a response from the boat."

L23

LOA 7.18 m, Beam 2.4 m, Draft 1.3 m, 1,300 kg, 27.7 m² sail area. Designed by Lars Olsen in 1975. Some 400 L23's were built.

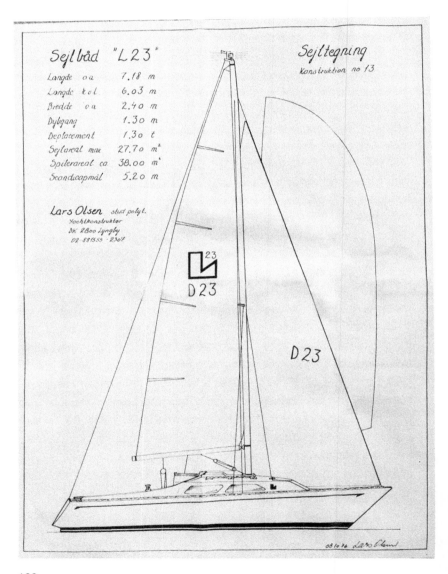

Anders Lund tells about his L23 Llingen: "As a cruising yacht the L23 is a small boat these days. But it is handled and fits in with ease and doesn't draw much water either. So it is well suited for protected waters and small boat harbours. You can always find a berth or a place to moor, when you get to your port of call. It is spacious for its size, and you sit really well in the cabin. The cabin table slides all the way to the coachroof allowing much more room in the cabin when not in use. The berths aren't too long, as there are no quarter berths. The settee berths are 180 respectively 185 cm. in length and the forepeak 175 cm, which one should take into consideration. I have mattresses extending all the way to the hullside, making the berths wide enough to sleep comfortably. But it varies a lot from boat to boat. It is furbished with a pantry, a small sink and a shelf to port next to the companionway and a chart table and a cabinet to starboard. It has a lovely big safe and deep cockpit with good sitting comfort."

"It's a very simple boat to sail. It takes strong winds in a good seakindly way and offers excellent sailing performance; it is fast for its size, works effeciently to windward and really sails well in light airs. The standard sail configuration doesn't even include a reef in the main. But I do reef in 20-24 knots of wind, if I have to beat against it for a long time - but otherwise, I don't. Many sail with a furling headsail, if they are more into cruising than racing. The L23 is still a one design class and organises its own Danish championship. There is an active class organisation and a helpful facebook group. Twice a year, trim weekends are held, offering training in all things sailing. As a newcomer, one is typically matched with people, who know how to sail the boats. And you also learn a lot about racing. The participants have loads of fun even in the back of the field of contestants. And yet we fight to win of course."

Leisure 17

LOA 5.18 m, Beam 2.13 m, Draft 0.97 m, 670 kg, 17 m² sail area. Designed by Arthur Howard in 1967. An impressive 3,400 boats were built.

The coachroof isn't exactly classically beautiful, but the interior layout and space is proportional to its size quite sensible and well suited for two people with modest accommodation demands. The little nutshell will bob its way over the swell and get her crew safely to their destination. In 1968 the German sailor John Adam crossed the Atlantic in a Leisure 17. Exhausted he fell asleep at a decisive time and beached the boat on a Cuban shore and endured prison for several months, before the authorities finally gave up their charges of espionage. They let him go but kept the boat.

A "dried out" Leisure 17 with bilge keels
Photo: From Wikipedia, Public domain. Author: Jakfei

Personally I have dreamed of getting a Leisure 17 with bilge keels (65 cm. draft) on a trailer for launching anywhere, where there's a slip or a self operated pivoting crane and go exploring nearby coasts and shoal waters, maybe up a creek or island hopping in the southern Funen Archipelago.

The German Yacht Magazin recently tested an old Leisure 17 on their Youtube channel and gave it a rather good review in relation to sailing performance and functional quality. Though the marketing department promoted it as a boat for a family of two adults and two children, very few would actually accept to live more than two adults on a short cruise. Or one adult and a couple of children.

From the Cobramold marketing of Leisure 17

Leisure 22

LOA 6.71 m, Beam 2.39 m, Draft 1.19 m, 1,495 kg, 26,5 m^2 sail area. Standing headroom 1.73 m. Designed by Graham Caddick in 1970. 200 Leisure 22 and even more Leisure 23 were built.

Leisure 22 from Cobramold marketing material.

Claes Molin tells the story of his 15 year old son Frederik, who was given a Leisure 22 by an elderly man, who was unable to keep sailing his boat. Claes and Frederik spent a lot of hours refitting it. "It's a really fun boat to sail. In the beginning we could only make it go 4-4.5 knots with old baggy sails, but after Frederik sewed himself a new foresail at OneSails for the boat and increased the sail area 30%, we logged 7-7.5 knots to windward - also thanks to a better trim. The boat is easy to sail. There are two winches, and everything is very simple. It is really dry to sail due to the flare in the bow and the coachroof. At the cost of some of the forward visibility. It is so tiny, yet it sails like a bigger boat, and it's turning radius isn't that big in spite of it's fin keel."

"The interior layout of the boat is incredibly well designed - almost like a caravan put into a boat. There is a quarter berth to port. On the starboard side you have a dinette seating for four with a table, which can be lowered and transformed into a bed for 1.5 persons. The v-berth in the forepeak fits an adult and a child very well. The cabin layout works very well, when we sit and drink coffee. There is a clever chart drawer under the table, and every inch is used to its potential. There is an incredible amount of stowage space. The inbuilt guiding paths for cables etc. is ingenious. However, the Leisure is not very well suited for a sprayhood. The coachroof is tall, and you walk over the coachroof and not the side deck when moving from cockpit to foredeck."

Leisure 23

LOA 6.90 m, Beam 2.39 m, Draft 1.19 m, 1,841 kg, 25.1 m² sail area. Standing headroom 1.75 m. Designed by Frank Pryor in 1973. 900 boats were built.

Leisure 23 was the successor of the popular Leisure 22 with similar design features and interior layout and was an instant success. With standing headroom and a spacious cabin, it also offered a dinette to starboard and a pantry to port in longitudal direction. The table can be lowered and the seating arrangement turned into a double berth.

The boat's reputation is one of very good sailing characteristics and it is still a sought after second hand boat despite the massive drop in prices on all old boats. The Leisure 23 is a typical British classic GRP yacht of the era. At a later stage the designers renewed the looks to a more modern wedge shaped coachoroof and abandoned the predominant two step coachroof of the 1960's and early 1970's. The wedge shaped type were clearly distinguishable with an "SL" added to the number.

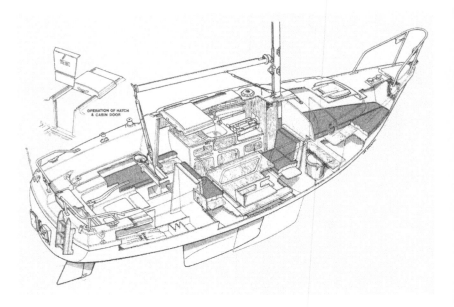

From the Leisure 23 brochure.
with permission from the Leisure Owners Association

The LM22 from the LM brochure. With permission from Lene Mi Ran, LM Windpower

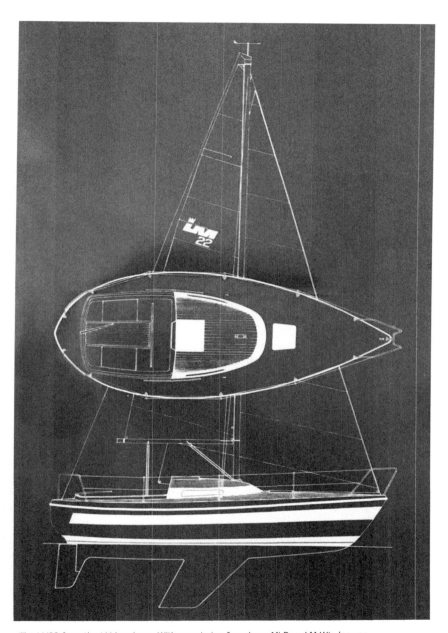

The LM22 from the LM brochure. With permission from Lene Mi Ran, LM Windpower

LM22

LOA 6.7 m, Beam 2.64 m, Draft 1.3 m, 1,600 kg, 27.5 m^2 sail area. Standing headroom 1.6 m. Designed by Bent Juul Andersen in 1975. Some 270 boats were built.

LM22 is a harmonious small but very roomy sailboat with a distinct kinship with the renowned LM motor sailers. It shares the rounded stern of the traditional fishing boats with its motor sailer siblings. But technically I would group it with the double enders. It was a huge success and is easily found in the brokerage market.

The LM22 of Lars Ekelunds

Lars Ekelund of Skovshoved tells about his boat: "I've had my LM22 for some 10-15 years and sailed it a lot. It isn't exactly a beautiful boat with elegant lines like commonly accepted classic beautiful boats. But it sails far better, than you would expect of it. It is very dry to sail and isn't thrown on its beam ends in a squall. The underwater lines resemble those of the 27 ft. Grinde. It offers a lot of living space for its size. The spacious accomodations and the sailing performance compared to much larger boats are far better than I imagined. The LM22 must be reefed in time and quickly achieves a steady 5.5 knots. I use an elastic chord as a self steering aid, which works fine abeam and upwind. I have a 6 HP outboard engine with a drop-down bracket, and it is a really good solution. I happily set out for both the island Anholt and Gothenburg in the Skagerak. It feels far safer than even far bigger boats, I have sailed. Mostly we cruise with a crew of two, for which it is very well suited. Three is alright, if you are not too demanding in terms of space. We have a toilet installed, and it would be wonderful also to have a cockpit tent and sprayhood, but I've actually done alright without them so far. I cook on a Trangia or small alcohol stove in the cockpit, where we also have a nice cockpit table, which is a really smart system. The cabin table can be lowered and transformed into a large berth, but I actually never used it. Instead of quarter berths, it has two giant stowage compartments. The berths are a fraction too short. I am 190 cm and I'm just able to lie in the saloon or the forepeak. There is so much stowage space, which you then tend to fill with all sorts of unnecessary stuff. The companionway hatch is tilted for opening, and that is the one thing, I am less happy about. It steers like a go-cart and turns on a plate with its big rudder and the small skeg in front of it. It is a perfectly trouble free boat, and I'm still a very happy LM22 owner and potential dreams about something bigger never really materialise."

Even Leif Frank from Fredericia, who until recently sailed a Jeanneau Fantasia 27 is happy about his newly acquired LM22: "I am very pleased with the boat and surprised, just how well it sails and how stable it is. The LM22 is incredibly well built to high craftman's standards." Following a divorce, Leif found an LM22 in which he could continue his sailing life both singlehanded and with his daughters. Though used to sailing, it was important for him, that the new boat would feel safe for them to sail in. "I have been on a three day cruise in it, but it is maybe a triffle too small for me, as I have been accustomed to standing headroom. So I gather, I will primarily take her for shorter cruises and daysailing to Middelfart, Bogense and southbound in the Lillebælt. It feels very safe with its great lead keel stability and wide beam compared to its overall length. It isn't thrown on its beam ends but calmly heels over at first and then rightens quite calmly again. It is a delightful boat, and it sails way better than the old one."

The LM22 of Leif Frank: The spacious cockpit with the traveller in front of the companionway.

Plenty of elbow room in the cabin. As the boat is designed without a main bulkhead, the open layout gives you a feeling of lots of space, light and air won below.

Photos: Leif Frank

Lynæs 14

LOA 4.65 m, Beam 1.88 m, Draft 0.5 m, 500 kg, 11.5 m² sail area. Designed by Ole Jensen and Christian Madsen. We find the Lynæs 14 or Lynæs Junior in the lowest end of the pocket cruising scale. It is a microscopic double ended keelboat with a minute cuddy cabin and two berths down below.

Two Lynæs 14's in the port of Marstal

Søren Simonsen tells about his Lynæs 14: "I grew up in Hundested (at the north coast of Zealand) and spent my childhood years in Lynæs Sailing Club. After the first years in the Optimist dinghy, I was allowed to sail the Lynæs dinghies (open 14 footers). Within a short time we were allowed to just take a dinghy out with a friend. The wonderful thing about being part of a sailing club is, that you are given the opportunity to begin sailing the boat yourself. The boat is so good-natured to sail on the Isefjord, for which it was designed as a fishing boat. The choppy seas often encountered on the Isefjord is spread to the sides by the bow rather than taking it over the stem. When I moved to Ho Bay close to Esbjerg in West Jutland, I hadn't sailed a Lynæs dinghy for many years. Twice a day, there isn't any water in the bay and otherwise very shallow water. I bought a Lynæs 14 and had it on a mooring for our family. You can crawl into the cabin and sit up. There is room for two under the coachroof. I had a boom tent for it, and it was simply a perfect dinghy for sailing. It isn't very far to the opposite side of the bay for an outing with the children, and it is easy to mess about with it. I also kept it on a trailer and once launched it in Hov, for us to embark on a vacation to the island Tunø in East Jutland. We lived in a tent on the beach camping and kept the boat at anchor for a fortnight."

"Its sailing performance is very good. It is so easy to handle, the jib isn't very large, and the boat simply is easy to get along with. It only has a low keelplank and some ballast, yet it effortlessly achieves 50-55 degrees to the wind. You really have a feeling of sitting down by the water."

Søren Høyer also sails a Lynæs 14 and he is an incarnated pocket skipper and the moderator of the facebook group Dansk Pocket Yacht Club, a small-boat community. He explains about the picture left:

"The bowsprit I installed this year is great improvement, and I recommend it to all those sailing short beamy boats."

Lynæs 18

LOA 5.85 m, Beam 2.36 m, Draft 1.03 m, 17 m² sail area, 1,275 kg. Double ender designed by Ole Jensen and Christian Madsen in 1967.

Svend Billesbølle circumnavigated the globe in this boat type and wrote a fascinating book about it. Despite its plump old-fashioned looks, the sailing characteristics are convincing, and it is quite simply the boat to take you anywhere you want to go.

The tiny Marieholm boat by Olle Enderlein is a genuine pocket cruiser. From the brochure of the Marieholm AC20. Made available by Claes Andersson.

Marieholm S20 / MS20 / AC20

LOA 6,0 m, Beam 2,2 m, Draft 0,9 m, 1.250 kg, 17 m² sail area. MS20 was designed by Olle Enderlein in 1971 with the addition of AC20 and S20 in 1975 and 1976. In total 1,150 boats were built: S for sailboat, MS for motor sailer and AC for aft cabin. Olle Enderlein succeeded in creating a small boat with an honest level of cruising comfort for two and a large functional cockpit with a sprayhood, offering good protection in foul weather. The boat displays fashionably good sailing characteristics for it's size and is a small boat on it's own terms and not a big boat squeezed into a tiny format. Above all, it is a pretty and harmonic boat with fine lines, accentuated in the two "clinker" lines in the hull making it stand out in the crowd. The little Marieholm is in the slightly heavy class of trailer sailers but perfect for outings and experiences in homely waters. In the Norrköping Sailing Society, the sailing school uses Marieholm MS20's.

Marieholm MS20 of Norrköping Sailing Society. Photographer: Håkan Wahren

Olle Enderlein was quoted for this design philosophy: "Beautiful boats sail well," which he has repeatedly proven with many of his successful designs, like the Hallberg Rassy series and the double ender OE32.

Marieholm AC20 off Lysekil in 2005. Photograph: Claes Andersson

Maxi 68

LOA 6.80 m, Beam 2.40 m, Draft 1.28 m, 1,550 kg, 25 m² sail area. Designed by Pelle Petterson in 1976. A total of 1,250 boats were built. An immensely popular first family boat in the mid seventies. More than 16,000 classic Maxi boats were built.

Bjarne Jensen sails his Maxi 68 as a husband-and-wife boat. They don't fancy having crew onboard, if they are to spend the night. There must be room to spare for the gear. "The Maxi is just as easy to singlehand as the Hurley 22 I used to sail. It is a fine cruising yacht, though proper stowage space is scarce.

Bjarne serving dinner in the officers' mess onboard his Maxi 68

The stowage compartments under the bunks are quickly filled. The forecastle is Randi's space on one side and reserved for travelling bags on the other. There is so much more room below compared to the Hurley, we sailed earlier. Cooking is done on a small gas stove, and it works very fine. We only cook in port and in fine weather. We have a sprayhood, and I am very grateful for it. I have considered to add a tarpaulin to place over the boom. We mostly dine in the cabin below. There is plenty of room for it, and we seldomly use the cockpit table. This years summer cruise had Fjällbacka on the Swedish west coast as the final destination. Otherwise, we sail a lot in Lillebælt during the season, as we are berthed in Middelfart, and I have a job that enables me to do it. But we also visited Aarhus several times as well as Kalundborg, Langeland, Ærø and Sønderborg. Randi actually doesn't care, where we are sailing. She just wants to be on the boat."

For sailing long distances, you need a bit of luck with the wind. The Maxi of Bjarne is equipped with a standard mainsail and a high aspect 110% genoa. "It doesn't sail very fast in light airs. It really likes flat water and a 14-18 knot

Maxi 68 "Havblik den Vældige" Photo: Henrik Ladegaard.

wind. In a seaway and a strong wind, it really takes a beating because of its flat bottom. Therefore, I take a reef early."

The depicted Maxi 68 (on this and the previous page) is not the boat of Bjarne but courtesy of Henrik Ladegaard. The boat is very well furbished and presentable.

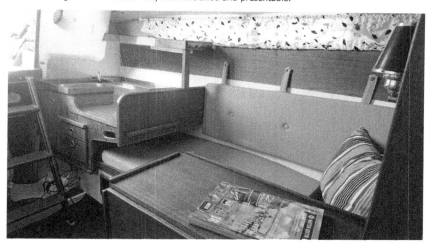

Maxi 77

LOA 7.70 m, Beam 2.50 m, Draft 1.45 m, 2,000 kg, 34 m² sail area. Designed by Pelle Petterson. The Maxi 77 was the first boat of the Maxi-series, and between 1971 and 1983 nearly 4,000 boats were built. It is one of the greatest successes of the Maxi boat yard and to this day still a highly popular first boat. In the 1970's it defined the concept of a typical family boat. It is very well furnished with great sailing performance. Only a few boat types have been built in equaly impressive numbers.

Maxi 77 "Tøsen" of Faaborg. Photo: Ulla Westermann.

Neptun 20

LOA 6.00 m, Beam 2.30 m, Draft 0.50/1.00 m, 950 kg, 23 m². Standing headroom with collapsible coachroof 1.77/1.40 m. Designed in 1973 by Anton Miglitsch. 1,900 boats were built until 1982.

Neptun 20 with its detachable coachroof. Photo: Courtesy of Pascal Ernst, Neptun Yachts.

The Neptun yard was one of the biggest boat-producers in Germany in the 1960's and 70's. There was a huge range of different sailing boat types from 17 to 32 ft. The yard still exists and provides new boats, spareparts, restoration and technical support.

The Neptun 20 was developed to offer a smaller and more affordable boat than her bigger sister the Neptun 22. Different from other boats in this class it was constructed with a centerboard built in a shallow ballast keel. Its a compromise between a keelboat and a true Jollenkreuzer with only a centerboard and demonstrates Neptun's approach to building safe cruising boats.

The yacht offers quite good accomodation for its size thanks to the lifting cabin top with sides in orange canvas. It also offers decent if not impressive sailing performance. So for pottering about on lakes or shorter coastal passages it is quite sufficient. We have met a well maintained Neptun 20 on several occasions during a summer cruise in Schleswig-Holstein with a singlehand skipper at the helm. The looks are classic, and with its campervan rooftop there is something utterly charming about the little time capsule of the 70's.

With 7,000 built, the Neptun 22 holds the German record for most production to date. It is still a very popular trailer sailer. Photo: Courtesy of Pascal Ernst, Neptun Yachts.

Neptun 22

LOA 6.80 m, Beam 2.40 m, Draft 0.55/1.05 m, 1.200 kg, 20 m². MkI designed in 1966 by Anton Miglitsch. Mk II designed by Lothar Leichtfuß in 1973, LOA 6,95 m, Beam 2,50 m.

7,000 boats were built in total by different boatyards under the name of Neptun 22 and M22 untill 1984, which is an amazing achievement.

The MkI by Miglisch was in production until 1974 and build in 2,300 examples. It was equiped with an engine-dwell and since 1973 with a canvas lift-top like the Neptun 20.

In 1973 the new MkII Version was given a totally different look with its Backdecker design. The broad deck allows more space down below, but at the expense of its classical profile. Both versions are build with either a shallow ballast keel and a built-in centerboard or with a finkeel.

The small Neptun boats from Germany really defined the scene of the common man's cruiser in the early years of GRP pleasure boating. Old reviews speak of quite decent sailing performance and dinghylike underwater hull. The Mk1 Version is said to offer better sailing performance.

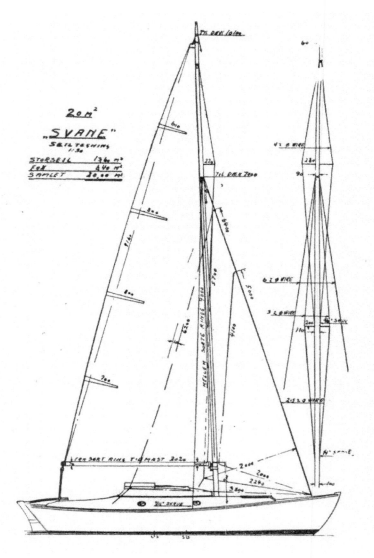

Entry A and winner of joint 2nd prize for the Nordic Folkboat was this design by renowned Danish naval architect Knud Olsen, who incidentally built Folkboat No.1 in Denmark. Knud Olsen was also the designer of the OK Dinghy, which won widespread international success as well as the whole range of Bandholm boats. See also the description of Bandholm 24 in this book.

Drawing from Sejl & Motor 1941 Courtesy of Søren Øverup, publisher of Baadmagasinet.

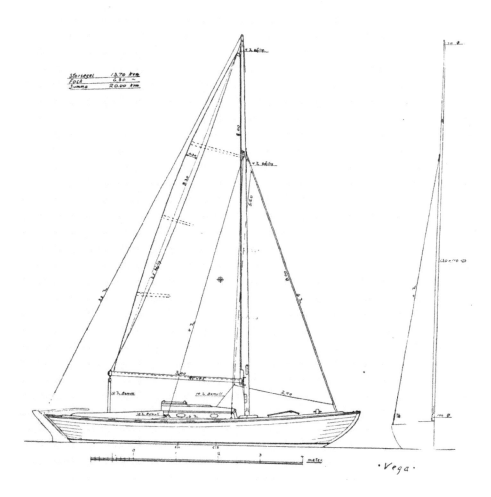

·Vega·

Entry B and joint winner of the 2nd prize for the Nordic Folkboat was this design by renowned Norwegian-Swedish engineer Jacob M. Iversen, mostly known for his beautiful double enders.

Drawing from Sejl & Motor 1941 Courtesy of Søren Øverup, publisher of Baadmagasinet.

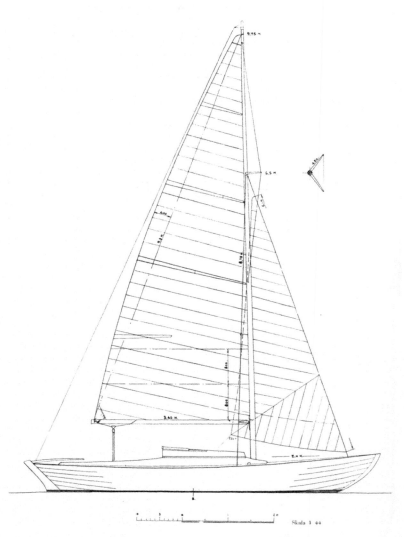

The final result was worked over and revised by designer and engineer Tord Sundén on the basis of the awarded joint 2nd place, 3rd and 4th entries in the design competition. He was never officially credited with the design of the Nordic Folkboat, and the Nordic Folkboat was officially presented in december 1941 with the above drawing in Sejl & Motor magazine.

Drawing from Sejl & Motor 1941, courtesy of Søren Øverup, publisher of Baadmagasinet.

Nordic Folkboat

LOA 7.68 m, Beam 2.2 m, Draft 1.2 m, 1,930 kg. 24 m^2 sail area. The design was completed by Tord Sundén commissioned by the Scandinavian Sailing Association in 1941 on the basis of the four winning design proposals. Built in GRP since 1977.

Far more than 4,000 Nordic Folboats have been built so far. It is sturdy, well built and offers excellent sailing performance with great appeal to sailors of the racing kind due to its strict one design and impressive numbers. They are excellent cruising boats with room for a small family. No other boat has set the standards for a lot of other boats like the Nordic Folkboat, and many boat types were designed with the same design and sailing qualities in mind. The boat is handled with great ease and sails so well, that it does not punish the inexperienced. It takes rough conditions in a stride and has accomplished many a long-distance and ocean passage. And it is actually simply the best at home in an evening race or cruising.

Many people perceive long keelers with a slender limited sail plan as sailing poorly and being heavy when coming about, like when going into port. But the Nordic Folkboat is a very vivid example of the contrary with its fine clinker lines and long narrow waterline; extremely good sailing characteristics and in reality fast for its size. Nowadays, you almost only see Folkboats coming into port under sail, letting the sails go and coming about to glide into their berths.

Many boats are described as safe and sailing well, but never truer than when speaking of the Nordic Folkboat. In Germany, it is part of a strong trend towards simple no-nonsense cruising boats for two people (sometimes even a small family) or as a daysailer. The Folkboat is "a boat you can wear." Everything is within reach, and you can fender off by hand when mooring and sail it in the spirit "never mind how foul the weather, full sails I always wear!" As it was communicated in the marketing propaganda of the 1970's.

The Folkboat DEN 909 "Alpi." Photograph: Flemming Palm

Folkboat "Alpi" in its summer cruise configuration with one big berth below. Photo: Flemming Palm

130

Flemming Palm sails the Folkboat Alpi of Kerteminde and explains: "The Folkboat is a long keeler, and that means, you don't have to worry if caught out in gale with your family. It is not being thrown about. It is directionally stable and safe if grounded. You feel very safe in a Folkboat. The cockpit is deep, and small children don't fall over the side. You walk from the cockpit into the cabin more or less at the same level. This means, that it is not self draining. Therefore, class rules require a 10 litre bucket onboard for bailing it. If it blows, you tighten the aft stay. It only carries a main and a jib, and this also renders a lot of safety and a sense of security. A single sailor will easily master it while tacking. People claim, that the Folkboat is slow, but you also see it overtake apparently faster boats like the Albin Express and X79's in long distance races like the Silver Rudder. It sails approximately 5.5 knots close hauled and achieves 36 degrees against the wind."

"We cruise our boat for a week every year. My wife and children aren't sailors, but they do enjoy the trip. It doesn't matter, what gales or foul weather we encounter. We won't get into trouble. We don't have any electrical installations onboard. We only have a battery driven lamp, a gas cooker and a portable fridge for a landbased powerchord. There are no sea cocks, so nothing can happen in that area. The rudder cannot fall off, as its construction strongly protects it. Trim and balance are perfect after 75 years of experience accumulated in the class. Anything which can break is dimensioned accordingly better. The wooden mast has a life span of approximately 25 years, whereas the aluminium mast has a much longer life expectancy and saves time on shore, for us to spend in the wet."

"One of the major advantages as a racing yachtsman are the big fleets of Folkboats across the country. You can get a pair of one year old sails for 1.100 €. New sails almost don't qualify as an actual investment. The cruising community enjoys this benefit as an added bonus. Therefore it is only right to support the association by subscribing to a membership." Flemming explains. He is a very active chairman of the northeast Funen Folkboat fleet.

"We see more and more young people in their twenties joining the class thanks to a youth project. It is a really good sign. We offer extra support by inviting them to sail with us, and we help them buy the right boat. Folkboats aren't for sale for long and Folkboats are raced on equal terms, whether it is dated 1976 or 2016. An old boat sails just as fast as a brand new one. And we have several suppliers of spares, making it cheap and easy to keep the boat in a good sailing condition."

Anders Lund tells the story of the picture above: "The Folkboat left Hjortø harbour with this somewhat unusual sail configuration one morning in a 4-8 knot wind while heading for Faaborg. I told the skipper, that my plan was to pass between the islands Drejø and Skarø on my way home to Fjellebroen, and he chose the same route. Later I passed by him with a slightly different set of sails: A main and a spinnaker. The wind increased during the morning to 8-12 knots, so it was a fine day for sailing. By the way, the route between Skarø and Drejø is fairly easy to navigate, coming from the Høje Stene fairlead. One should just start from the green light marker (a starboard side marker with a flash on a pole) north of Hjortø and pass close to Skarø, with an approximate course of 300^0-305^0."

"The experience got me thinking about, how many sailboats I encounter motoring in all sorts of weather. The Folkboat crew apparently spent a happy enjoyable time on the water and close to nature, because with the mainsail they would probably have sailed twice the speed, even with a boom tent hoisted as extra canvas."

"A fine way of acquiring more sailing hours is to expand your "window" by sailing in both lighter and heavier weather than usual. In light airs things go slower, so you plan for that. Arriving a little later doesn't really matter, and you also have the possibility to aim for a harbour nearer to you."

"For both strong and light airs the trim is important to accomplish a good and safe sailing, and it gives you better speed and in stronger winds less heel to trim sail and rig correctly. Expand your window little by little and get more and better hours under sail. And remember to enjoy the nature experience in their wake."

Polaris Drabant 26

LOA 7.8 m, Beam 2.4 m, Draft 1.42 m, 36.6 m² Sail area. 2,620 kg. Standing headroom 1.75 m. Designed by Gert Gerlach in 1971. The Polaris Drabant was a very popular family boat, and 312 were built in the period of 1971 to 1981. The Pd26 is an excellent cruising yacht for a family, which to this day makes it an attractive bargain. Being a representative of the upper end of the pocket cruising range, it offers comfort like bigger boats with the ease of handling of the smaller under sail and when mooring. It is designed with coachroof in two steps typical of the era, recognisable on so many boats of the 1970's.

The Pd26 offers decent berths for four adults and and a child. Gert Gerlach designed the boat for cruising and not as a race yacht but rather a natural successor of the Drabant 22. He truly exceeded the expectations by designing such an accomplished allround boat.

The Polaris Drabant can be seen in most ports. It is popular and hit the spot in the market for the smallest family boats. Photo: Martin Holm

Polaris Drabant 26
Designed by Gert Gerlach

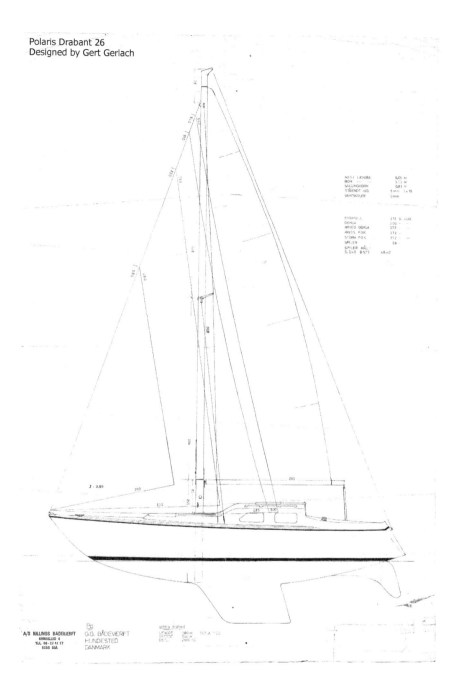

Sagitta 20

LOA 6.14 m, Beam 2.35 m, Draft 1.2 m, 1,700 kg. 26 m² sail area. Standing headroom 1.8 m. Designed by Sparkman & Stephens. 200 boats were built from 1969 to 1979. The cabin offers a cosy interior and no sliding hatch but an oval opening, you must snuggle through, which works very well in practice. It sails well and is safe with a well thought out layout for its size though somewhat compact.

Signet 20

LOA 6.04 m, Beam 2.03 m, Draft 0.91 m, 973 kg, 15,7 m² sail area. Designed by Ray Kaufmann in 1960 and built by Hurley Marine among others in the mid 1960's.

A fine specimen of a Signet 20 seen in the tiny port Boels Bro in Munkebo on Funen.

Sunwind 20

LOA 6.0 m, Beam 2.45 m, Draft 1.25 m, 1,500 kg, 21 m^2 sail area. Designed by Tord Sundén in 1970 as a small family boat for sailing on the North atlantic westcoast of Norway. 200 boats were built.

The Sunwind 20 is an unusually pretty little sailboat with lines and hullform of large sailboat in a small format. It was originally built in Norway under the name Sagawind, but later became the Sunwind 20 and was being built by the Nykra Boatyard in Finland. It is described as a stiff boat and a wonderful boat for learning to sail. A fine cruising yacht for two on longer trips or four on outings or a weekend. In short a great little sailboat.

A fine specimen of a Sunwind 20 with a "twinkle in the eye" following Greek inspiration belonging to Jim Quarnström, a Swedish sailor.

"I thrive with my little boat. I did a lot of yacht racing in an X95 among others, but this one suits me perfectly for getting on sea single-handed. Easily handled and safe."

Sunwind 26

LOA 7.8 m, Beam 2.6 m, Draft 1.5 m, 2,200 kg, 34 m^2 sail area. Designed by Tord Sundén in 1978. 350 boats were built.

Svendborg Senior

LOA 5.8 m, Beam 2.2 m, Draft 0.85 m, 16 m^2 sail area. 760 kg. Designed by E. Bjørn Jensen in 1968. approximately 200 boats were built over a period of 30 years. The boat was built for the sea scouts as a replacement for the Aalborg Dinghy designed by Aage Utzon.

Four Svendborg Senior boats from the Sea Scouts troop Gry in Svanemøllen. Photo: Sea Scouts Denmark

Bertram, who earlier on in this chapter told about his Albin Viggen, is a sea scout trainer in Svanemøllen, from where they sail four Svendborg Seniors: "When I was a boy , we sailed on weekend trips to flakfortet (one of three old fortifications of Copenhagen dating back to the years before WW1) with the Svendborg Senior boats. The crews consisted of six 12-13 year old boys in each boat. One in the cockpit, one on deck, one in each quarter berth, one in the bow and one on the cabin floor. On the cabin floor, you could lie on top of

Svendborg Senior boats from the Seascouts troop Gry of Svanemøllen on tour.
Photo: Courtesy of Seascouts Denmark

all the kit bags level with the bunks. Cooking was done on two Trangia stoves, and the menu was pasta and meatsauce."

"It sails like a keelboat. It has an aft hinged rudder and steers like a dinghy. Also it is a fairly heavy boat and sails somewhat slowly. It can be trimmed to sail better, which makes it extremely good for learning to sail. And it is safe, pleasant to sail and has a calm movement pattern. It carries its genoa and spinnaker well." Bertram, head of the Sea Scout troop Gry explains.

With its shallow draft and safe sailing characteristics, the Svendborg Senior is an obvious choice as a pocket cruiser for small coastal exploring adventures in sounds and fjords. Though the boat offers room for 6 spirited sea scouts, the boat is actually more suitable for a singlehanded sailor, who appreciates the simple comfort of fine sailing characteristics, easy handling, sitting headroom and a boom tent. Or two outdoor lovers.

With its shallow draft, you can sail it onto the beach and wade in or sneak up a creek, cove or inlet, where others cannot. It can be tied to a pole near land or be moored on the smallest jetties and small boat harbours.

Varianta

LOA 6.50 m, Beam 2.10 m, Draft 0.7-1.0 m, 900 kg, 23 m². Designed in 1967 by E.G. van de Stadt. 4,000 boats were built by Dehler Yachtbau.

The Varianta was - in addition to the FAM and the Neptun 20/22 - the most popular pocket-cruiser in Germany in the 1970's. There are three versions of the boat on the market:

The first Varianta K3 (1969-1972, No. 1 - 275) was an innovative „multitool." The dinghy hull was provided with a removable hardtop made of GRP. The boat can be sailed as an open dinghy or used for holiday cruises as a Jollenkreuzer with very basic comfort under deck.

More comfort and safety is offered by the Varianta K4 (1969-1972, No. 276-1075) with a solid cabin and a self draining cockpit.

The following Varianta 65 (1972-1982, No. 1076 - 4000) was a redesigned K4 with a clear focus on cruising qualities. Cabin and cockpit appear roomier than the K4, whereas the older sister offers better sailing performance.

Both the K4 and 65 are great sailboats and offer a lot of safety for coastal cruising due to their centerboard construction.

Varianta 65 in the Greifswalder Bodden. Creative Commons Attribution-Share Alike 4.0 International license. Photo by: Zeichner01

The Varianta story doesn't end with the 65. In 1994, the Dehler Yachtbau launched the Dehler 18 "Rotkäppchen" (means „Red Riding Hood"), as an entry model for their sailboat series. "Rotkäppchen" was a typical Dehler Yacht with lots of innovative ideas and details of construction. Production ended quite soon, because it didn't sell very well.

In 2009 Hanse Yachts launched the Dehler 18 (Design Judel & Vrolijk) as a follower for the Dehler "Rotkäppchen." Unlike the "Rotkäppchen," the Dehler 18 was sold quite cheap to attract younger buyers for the bigger Hanse range of bigger boats, but the standard specifications were poor, and the boat could only be delivered in two fixed keel versions, which makes trailering unnecessarily complicated.

In 2014 production ended after only 299 boats had been built.

Vivacity 20

LOA 6.1 m, Beam 2.13 m, Draft 0.99 m, 20 m^2 sail area. 839 kg. A redesign by D. C. Pollard in 1967 as an extended edition of the Alacrity 19, designed by Peter Stevenson in 1960. 825 of these British golden age GRP boats were built by Hurley Marine among others.

15. MODERN POCKET CRUISERS

Though the primary tendency in today's market is ever bigger boats, and a 35 footer is considered small, quite a few pocket cruisers are still being designed and built.

Bayraider Expedition 20

LOA 6.05 m, Beam 2.05 m, Draft 0.25/1.42 m, 520 kg. 17,7 m^2 sail area. Designed by Matt Newland of Swallow Yachts. The boat is a typical "raid boat" or daysailer with cruising potential in simplistic camping comfort.

It is ballasted partly by a leaded swing keel, partly by self flooding water tanks, that are drainable by hand or an electric pump. You can sail fast and fun unballasted or work your way in a headwind in comfort and safety with filled tanks. This makes it particularly suitable for the tough conditions reigning coastal Britain with big tidal differences and strong currents.

The rig is made of carbon fibre and consists of a main and mizzen mast. The 2 m^2 mizzen sail enables the skipper to drop the mainsail in gale force winds and still sail both fast and stable with a jib and mizzen. Owners described how they entered a harbour in a gale force wind and were met with horrified disbelief by people on shore, whereas they themselves never experienced it anywhere near horrifying. The philosophy of two-masted English raid boats is to maintain a balance in the sail plan under all conditions and being able to reduce the sail area easily.

The boat has an enormeous cockpit and sitting room for two adults and two children down below. A large collapsible sprayhood and a cockpit tent are optional. Cooking is done in the cockpit on a camping stove. The outboard is situated in a well aft and can be tilted out of the water while sailing, and the hole closed by clever lamels. The Bayraider Expedition could follow Wayfarers and other open cruising dinghies right on to the beach for a rest or a picnic.

Bayraider Expedition 20 with asymmetric spinnaker, main and mizzen. Swallow Yachts project a successful mix between classic appearance and modern performance thanks to low weight and center of gravity combined with water ballast. Photo: Matt Newland, Swallow Yachts

The choice of a carbon rig not only ensures the right balance between weight and sail area, the highest achievable performance and a safe and comfortable passage under most conditions. It also makes launching and rigging highly efficient. The design is both elegant and sporty with distinct inspiration from traditional work boats.

Baycruiser 23 at anchor. Photo: Matt Newland, Swallow Yachts

Baycruiser 23

LOA 6.98 m, Beam 2.36 m, Draft 0.3/1.5 m, 850 kg. 24.2 m² sail area. Designed by Matt newland.

BC23 is a British piece of ingenuity. The British may be known to be very conservative, but the BC23 is an example of design based on tradition and the looks of work boats of the past but combined with quite fresh sailing performance of a modern boat. Water ballast, swing keel and carbon fibre masts contribute to create great stability without sacrificing speed and performance. BC23 is an unusally pretty boat and has become a big success in just a few years. It can be sailed in cruising mode with 500 kg of water ballast or in sports mode with empty tanks and an asymmetrical spinnaker. It has a thought through cabin layout and is furnished with white painted plank structured plywood in the workboat style and a light oak trim. With its shallow draft, it is both trailerable and beachable.

Raid boats

Swallow Yachts refer to their boats as "raid boats." But what does the term actually mean? A raid is a sail-and-oar event for small craft, a relaxed race on a predefined stretch of coast.

In a broad sense a raid is a social gathering for small shallow draft boats to sail together and explore parts of a coastal line, while laying a distance in their wake in stages of one or more days. Typically, they will anchor for lunch underway or beach the boats, and the day's destination is both an overnighting site and the setting of a meat-and-eat between crews. These kind of rallies or raids are quite popular in Britain and France, where the annual "Semaine de Golfe" in Golfe du Morbihan i Brittany is the host of a gigantic sailing event for boats of all sizes and varieties.

Moored in layers for "cream tea" underway: Two Bayraider Expedition 20, two Bayraider 20 and on the outside a Baycruiser 23. Photo: Matt Newland, Swallow Yachts

Cornish Shrimper 19

LOA 5.87 m, (6.86 m, with a bowsprit), Beam 2.19 m, Draft 0.46/1.22 m, 1,065 kg, 18 m² sail area. Can be delivered with either an outboard well or an inboard 9 hp Yanmar diesel. Since 1979 more than 1,100 Cornish Shrimper 19 were built.

Cornish Shrimper 19 "Henrietta" of Falmouth. Photo: Shrimper Owners Association, Falmouth.

It's a real cosy looker of a boat to potter about in with all the luxury and comfort imaginable you could squeeze into a 19 foot sailboat and suitable for elderly couples. But looks are deceiving: Elderly couples aren't what they used to be, and they rather favour to race their beautiful "old gaffer" as well take it on shorter and longer cruises with no comfort spared. Being a fairly heavy boat, it takes a somewhat beefy car to trail it. But even as a trailer sailer, it offers an abundance of freedom, to those with too little time, prefering to

Cornish Shrimper 19 "Henrietta" af Falmouth. Foto: Shrimper Owners Association, Falmouth.

launch it, every time they go sailing. Launching and rigging for these types of small boats typically takes around 30-60 minutes.

Cornish Crabbers are classic looking sturdy cruising boats for a singlehander or a couple in comfort with such an immense popularity, that they are widely raced too in Britain.

The Jollenkreuzer, a somehow German speciality

As Germany has a large treasure of coastal waters under tidal influence facing the North Sea with its many estuaries, demanding conditions for sailing boats making low or variable draft an obvious choice. Also inshore lakes and rivers are often too shallow for keelboats.

Since the 1920's a large variety of so called "Jollenkreuzer" spread all over inshore and coastal waters. Jollenkreuzer basically means „dinghy with a cabin," a boat with a centerboard and some accomodation. The missing keel-weight means, that these boats can capsize. Most of them are equipped with buoyancy bodies and won´t sink in case of capsize. One of the benefits of the missing keel is - beside low draft - easy launch and recovery as a trailer boat. These boats don´t need a water-berth during the season.

Its mainly a construction class distinguished by sail area (15, 16, 20, 25, 30 m²) and some rules concerning weight and measurement. The first Jollenkreuzer were made of wood or steel, later GRP emerged in boat classes too, and some very popular boat types built in numbers deserve to be recognised. In their total amount, the Jollenkreuzer represent the majority of sailing vessels in Germany.

Klepper FAM 17 - Jollenkreuzer

LOA 5.4 m, Beam 2.05 m, Draft 0.23/1.40 m, 435 kg, 19 m² sail area. Designed by Uwe Mares and Hubert Raudaschl in 1969. More than 2,500 boats have been built. The boat is still in production by Bootsbau Gruben at the Bodensee.

The German word for this type of dinghy-like boat with a lid on it or a cuddy cabin is "Backdecker." The cabin-roof is extended to the hullside with no side decks beside the roof.

Klepper FAM is easy to trail and launch. Photo: Courtesy of Henrik Dinesen.

It represents one of the absolute smallest of pocket yachts with accomodation being a place to rest and sleep. Throughout its history, it has been immensely popular as the travel light common man's trailerable access to the sea or any of the big lakes and rivers of Germany. It is fair to say, that it holds a place in the German self perception, when it comes to sailing small craft.

There is an active class organisation, FAMAS Deutschland e. V. and an active racing scene as well as organised rallies and meets for the cruising minded pocket skippers. It carries a fair amount of canvas for its size indicating a rather sporting performance. The boat is unsinkable, but being a dinghy with a ballasted centerboard it can capsize in very rough conditions. The main can be reefed.

What the FAM can do!

His passion for sailing began in the summer of 1971 with the FAM, Klaus Hinrichsen from Flensburg explains. This is his story:

Family photo: Courtesy of Klaus Hinrichsen.

"I had just turned 14 and had hardly seen a sailboat in my life. We knew the Baltic Sea from bathing and swimming in the summer and from many tours with the ferry from Gelting Mole to Sønderborg and Faaborg in Denmark."

"In 1970 Gelting Yacht Club (GYC) was founded, and in winter the first theoretical sailing course was offered for newbies. In spring 1971 most club members travelled to Hamburg on a chartered bus with the intention to look for a suitable boat at the Hamburg boatshow."

"We, that was my older brother and me, my father and a colleague and his three children participated enthusiastically together and full of expectations. Already at the boatshow, our fathers decided to purchase a FAM in joint ownership. No doubt, this decision was fuelled by a very industrious neighbour; who not only was the first commodore of the new sailing club but also the local sales-representive for all types of Klepper boats - manufacturer of the FAM."

"So now we were eleven people sharing the new boat, which was moored in the buoy field, along with some 40 other sailboats, mostly orange-white boats from Klepper like Jeton, Trainer, FAM, Traveler and Okton. Our FAM was named CANINUS (canine tooth), because our fathers were dentists. Our pastor, also a new FAM owner, gave us practical sail training after confirmation class, and within a few weeks we were able and allowed to sail in the Gelting Bay alone and sometimes even to nearby Danish harbours like Sønderborg or Høruphav."

"The following year our FAM was by far the most sailed boat in the region, while we quickly learned to appreciate the amazing performance and strengths of the small sailboat. We loved to sail it, even in strong winds. Like a fast trip to Sønderborg, eating hot dogs and softice there and back to Gelting. The FAM was - if reefed - surprisingly resilient with four people on the cockpit edge and the ballast sword rolled down."

"In the morning at school, we agreed who could go sailing with whom in the afternoon and for how many girlfriends and friends there would be room. The generous cockpit of the FAM was enormously good. It was not uncommon for us to have four or more people on board. The okay from our parents came with our promise to do the homework on board. In practice it was rarely - in fact never done.... (there was still time in the morning on the bus for homework, at least for copying). The FAM just wasn't a very suitable replacement for an office-desk."

"Four years later a second FAM was bought. Now each family had their own sailboat, and also additionally equipped with genoa and spinnaker. We frequently loaded the FAM with sleeping bags, toast bread and Nasi Goreng from Aldi, beers and a guitar and sailed on the bay or to the Geltinger Birk, where we pulled the FAM onto the beach. There we met with friends in the evening to eat, drink, smoke, chatter and swim. In the evening we sang songs by Bob Dylan, Leonard Cohen, Joan Baez, Hannes Wader and the Beatles, sitting around the campfire."

"If you had a FAM, you didn't have to put up a tarpaulin over the boom or set up a cockpit tent. Four people could sleep in the bunks. We enjoyed the independence and freedom away from home."

"In the fall of 1974 I took a trip with three friends to circumnavigate Als and Ærø. Before hitting the bunks, the beer and food boxes had to be piled up in the cockpit. It was pretty tight and stuffy, but it worked. Smoking was only allowed in the open hatch. During my studies I sailed as much as possible and undertook further trips. An adventurous five week trip lead my friend and me around the islands of Funen and Zealand up to the Swedish west coast."

"In 1985 my new girlfriend Antje immediately joined in the delight of sailing with me and the FAM. After several daytrips and weekend tours during the summer of 1986, we made a voyage in the archipelago south of Funen, covering the the South Zealand Småland fairway and the islands Falster and Møn. Antje just loved sailing, the Danish isles and probably also me. We got along very well together on this little boat, and we got married in autumn 1986. The test sail was a complete success!"

Family photos: Courtesy of Klaus Hinrichsen.

154

"In 1989 we sold the FAM with a heavy heart. Meanwhile we were expecting our second child, had a house, garden, cat and dog. Neither of us could find enough time nor opportunity to go sailing. But my enthusiasm for sailing was intact, and I was able to take some time every year with friends to sail."

"In the following decade we bought bigger boats with more space, but everytime I see a FAM lying in the harbour I have to stop and recapture my memories. The FAM paved the way to sea for me and for sailing and I´m most grateful of that."

Sailart 19

LOA 5.7 m, Beam 2.5 m, Draft 0.6/1.3 m, 730 kg, 22 m² sail area.

It is described as a performance oriented pocket cruiser, also available in various configurations for singlehand sailors with self tacking jib respectively as a racing boat for a small crew. The looks are very modern and sporty with a slight negative bow, a chine aft and a built in small bowsprit for the spinnaker. With its low weight, it is trailerable even with smaller midsized family cars.

Sailart 19.
Photo: Frank Störck, Sailart

Sailart are sober modern small sailboats, and the name suggests emphasis on good sailing performance. Obvious for racing with simplistic cruising potential. They are fresh and sporty, succeeding in looking like compressed   siblings of far bigger proper yachts in easily handled and trailerable micro format.

Sailart 20

LOA 6.0 m, Beam 2.5 m, Draft 0.6/1.4 m, 820 kg, 17.8 m^2 sail area. The yard describes it as a comfortable and safe yacht with great hull stability, that will ensure the singlehand sailer the best conditions with its self tacking jib - even in rough weather. It is clearly targeted at the solo yachtsman. Down below it displays a fine finish, is well laid out and snug. With its modest weight it is trailerable with a mid sized family car. Sailart accomplished to give the 20 the looks of a "proper" yacht, and like her bigger sisters of 22 and 24 foot, she looks like a genuinely solid sailboat.

Sailart 20 in ankle depth off a beach in the Danish Limfjord.

Photo: Frank Störck, Sailart

Also check out:

Sailart 22

LOA 6.5 m, Beam 2.3 m, Draft 0.66/1.45 m, 1,100 kg, 24 m^2 sail area.

Sailart 24

LOA 7.40 m, Beam 2.5 m, Draft 0.95/1.3 m, 1,350 Kg, 24 m^2 sail area.

Seacamper IF

LOA 7.87 m, Beam 2.2 m, Draft 1.21 m, 2,150 kg, 31 m² sail area. The IF Boat was designed by Tord Sundén in 1966 and put back into production again in 2019 in a collaboration between dedicated IF-sailor Peter Grönlund of Seacamper in Berlin and the IF Owners Associations. It will be interesting to see the renaissance of Tord Sundén's giant success 50 years later, and what it will mean to the future of the class. The boat is currently being promoted at several IF-venues to creative positive public attention of the class and boat. The IF 2019 is an honest, solid cruising sailboat with simplistic comfort for dedicated sailors. It also addresses new sailing families set on the accomodations and functionality, the beautiful classic offers. Especially if you wish to buy a new boat with a more modest maintenance effort, rather than an old boat at a more affordable purchasing price but with higher running costs for sails and maintenance. Regardless of your choice, the IF now as then is an excellent choice of a small family yacht

Seacamper IF in her natural habitat: The Swedish skerries. Photo: Peter Grönlund, Seacamper.

Seacamper IF beating to windward. Photo: Peter Grönlund, Seacamper

Sunbeam 22.1

LOA 6.85 m, Beam 2.49 m, Draft 0.6/1.4 m, 1,300 kg, 28 m² sail area. The Sunbeam 22 was designed by E.G. van de Stadt in 1968 and has been built by Schöchl Yachtbau in Austria for more than 50 years. Since 2016 in the modernised version Sunbeam 22.1.

The boat looks great and seems very solid. The interior and layout are nicely carried out with a great finish, and with its swingkeel the boat is an excellent choice for the trailer-sailor with a bigger mid range family car for extended weekend cruises within a range of several hundred kilometers from the home port (or garage).

It's enjoyable to see an old popular construction being redesigned as a more contemporary representative of a small sailboat equally suited for daysailing

Sunbeam 22.1 Sporty and elegant. Photo: Courtesy of Sunbeam Yachts, Schöchl Yachtbau

on lakes as well as coastal hopping. The result seems very accomplished, and the build is smart and solid with a great finish.

Also look for:

Sunbeam 24.2

LOA 7.0 m, Beam 2.5 m, Draft 0.72/1.4 m, 1,420 kg, 32.5 m² sail area. Standing headroom 1.5 m. Designed by Georg Nissen, Schöchl Yachtbau in 2002.

Sunbeam 26.2

LOA 8.0 m, Beam 2.5 m, Draft 0.78/1.33 m, 2,250 kg, 34.5 m² sail area. Standing headroom 1.8 m.

16. MY PERSONAL POCKET CRUISER EXPERIENCE

For many years, I exclusively sailed dinghies. After several years without a boat and with small children, we moved to Kerteminde on the Island of Funen with only a short distance to the fjord and the Great Belt. I had an urge to get my first keelboat. I considered sailing boats like Hurley 18, Sailfish 18, Impala 20, Leisure 17, Carina 20 og Hurley 20.

One day in April 2001 I took my eldest son Emil (9 years old at the time) to Aarhus in Jutland to have a look at a Hurley 20 from 1969, which had been the family boat for four since it was built. It was standing on its bilge keels grey and sad looking in a barn. The cabin was filled with gear, original sails, old fenders, life vests, two fishing rods and a captains hat, along with a couple of rolls of toilet paper in the middle of the cabin table. Emil, who had dived in to explore the mess, decisively turned around and exclaimed: "Buy it Dad. Buy it." And so I did.

With great enthusiasm and support from Emil and his younger brother Oscar (6 years old) we cleared up the mess, cleaned up, polished and antifouled the boat in the course of three-four weeks and launched it. The children played fishermen and captains with the caps and fishing rods, as much as they helped with the work, and the boat became a great playing ground for us during and after the weeks on dry land.

The excitement was immense, as the boat was hauled up by the harbour crane and lowered into the water, being the wonderful little egg shell it was. I was terrified, as I motored her to her jetty for the first time. The outboard was a terribly noisy air cooled old Honda. I pottered just outside the harbour entrance with wife and kids and the mast lying on the coach roof and turned a couple of hundred metres out. In the middle of the harbour entrance, the engine failed and I sweat the sweat of anxiety, as I pulled the starting chord 20-30 times, before it roared once more, and we could dock in safety again.

Hurley 20

Underway in in a slight breeze from Romsø to Fynshoved with a stuffed
animal. Observe the Silva 33 parallel steering compass.

The Hurley 20 "Tulle"

LOA 6.09 m, Beam 2.16 m, Draft 0.99 m, Displacement 1,031 kg, 22.3 m² sail
area. Sitting headroom inside the cabin 1.27 m. Designed in 1967 by Ian L.
Anderson. 435 boats were built, quite a few of them to Denmark, where it is
quite commonly seen.

The accommodation consists of a v-berth in the forepeak and two settee/
quarter berths in the fairly roomy cabin. A well thought of detail is the
extractable table over the port quarter berth, serving both as a pantry table
and chart table. The pantry is placed midship. I built a cooker box to hold a
one burner camping stove with a pot on top, fitting the space between the
cockpit benches as well as the cabin floor while under way.

My friend Jørn and our youngest sons Oscar and Jonas on a daysail in the Hurley 20

At anchor in Korshavn (= Cross-harbour a quite common Danish and Scandinavian name)

The Hurley gave us lots of wonderful sailing experiences, sailing remarkably well in spite of its compressed proportions and compromising looks, shallow bilge keels and ancient old sails. And above all, it was astonishingly dry in a choppy sea, thanks to the volume and flare of the bow. The Hurley 20 rides just about everything off in a nutshell like seakindly manner.

My sailorfriend Jørn joined me in a boat community, and we had a wonderful sailing trip to Samsø with the two eldest of our total of four boys and a lot of small cosy outings with the two little ones back in the Bay of Kerteminde in the Great Belt.

After a couple of seasons, we sold the boat to Ray, an old British seadog heading back to the UK after many years of living in Denmark. He lived aboard on shore for several months in Kerteminde entertaining mates in his tiny pub, before floating the boat a little late in the season and heading for the Kiel Canal and the North Sea. I often wondered, what became of him and the boat, and I guess it probably was handed on to a new enthusiastic boat owner somewhere along the east coast of Britain.

First port of call in a foreign harbour on the island of Samsø. Our eldest sons Emil and Joachim. Great expectations on the foredeck!

The Spækhugger "Granit Gurli"

LOA 7.44 m, Beam 2.33 m, Draft 1.45 m, 2,300 kg, 40 m^2 sail area. Designed by Peter Bruun in 1969. 500 Spækhuggers were built. The boat is still in production.

In the course of the winter we looked at a couple of Spækhuggers and finally purchased Granit Gurli with sail number D165 in Sønderborg and sailed her back home to Kerteminde in the beginning of March in all kinds of weather. With frost at night and anything from becalmed to gale during the days. In two long days we sailed the 90 nautical miles with our more seasoned mate Steffen as professional moral support. After the trip he congratulated us on our hard earned skipper status. He later joined us as part owner. We learned a lot from our "sea-midwifery-passage," as the British call a transfer of a new ship to its home port. These kind of passages are something really special and exciting. Will she float or sink? Will the sails and gear stand the load all the way home? Granit Gurli was a former girls' racing yacht and had a pink waterline and pastel rope, which we found to be rather cool.

The Spækhugger is an amazing sailing machine and a decent cruising yacht with a reservation on account of its low sitting headroom just allowing you sit up straight and move through the narrow boat like a WW2 German u-boat crew. It sort of puts a point to the comfort of the accommodation, and we just loved it.

Our children grew up in the Spækhugger, and we had lots of good experiences together and individually. We had a barbecue on the jetty, while the children were fishing for crabs. I often induced the courage of my youngest always seasick Oscar with a promise of a sausage and bread, when we came ashore. Jørn, Steffen and I sailed on several occasions with four or five children and two adults for a week at a time. It was all fun and "hygge," but when we hit our bunks, there were children all over the place, and it was a bit of a puzzle to fit in. The Spækhugger forecastle has a wonderful large v-berth

My youngest son Oscar on a cruise in the Spækhugger

Oscar in the cabin and his mother with a favourite book on a fair wind cruise in the Spækhugger

with plenty of room for an adult and two children. You sleep so well arm in arm with children.

What makes the Spækhugger so special and gives it its quality of making it so safe for children is actually its low freebord. It may sound strange, but the closer to the water, the less scary it seems. And you get so much more out of the sailing experience. You can reach the water with your hands and play with a fishing net.

Supper onboard the Spækhugger was prepared on an Optimus parrafin stove, which was preheated with alcohol before opening the fuel valve. With Jørn as our permanently commissioned cook, supper was a true feast, and the appetite of the entire crew was a great recognition. The secret ingredient was cream and a solid meal. A true hit.

With or without the children, we enjoyed many pleasant outings and short cruises in the worn old workhorse. Today she sails under German flag with Berlin as her home port and has made a trip up the westcoast of Ireland after a comprehensive and magnificent restoration.

More than 500 Spækhuggers were built, and they make out an attractive racing scene to lots of young sailors in both Copenhagen and the regional capital of Jutland, Aarhus. The Spækhugger Owners Association put up a system for the refurbishment of old Spækhuggers and offers detailed descriptions on their home page spaekhugger.dk.

Our very first family cruise in the Spækhugger Granit Gurli. My wife Mette on deck duty. Ballen on Samsø island.

The Hurley 18 Oracle

LOA 5.63 m, Beam 2.03 m, Draft 0.99 m, 1,060 kg, 16,7 m² sail area. Sitting headroom in the cabin 1.22 m. Designed in 1963 by Ian L. Anderson as a scaled down version of Hurley 22, 377 boats were built by Hurley Marine until 1972, whereafter production was continued by different boat yards right up until 1986. In total more than 900 boats were built.

My youngest son Oscar, who had spent his childhood in a condition of seasickness, had developed a stomach for the sea at 20 - so much so that he fancied a boat of his own. I didn't think twice but ventured a secret plan with his brother Emil to acquire a tiny sailboat jointly. I found a fine Hurley 18 in Horsens on the east coast of Jutland, which we bought against the undivided resentment of my wife. For Easter of 2015 the three of us sailed the tiny boat

It takes a lot of gear for three grown men to make sea-midwifery passage in winter from Horsens in Jutland to Kerteminde via the island Endelave in a Hurley 18. It was a marvellous father-and-two-sons adventure.

to her new port in Kerteminde. The boat is in my perception a classically beautiful sailboat. It looks like a big yacht shrinked (quite a bit). There is just enough headroom for sitting, a pantry to port, a quarter berth to starboard and a v-berth, which transforms into a double berth. The Hurley 18 is a semi long keeled boat, initially slightly tender but rights herself quickly when picking up speed from a gust or increased wind. She sails well and feels secure and is in fact a microscopic thoroughbred coastal cruiser. Hurley 18 is well suited for the solo yachtsman for short and longer passages and great for weekend excursions - perhaps even for week long trips for two people prepared for a basic camping style comfort level.

The man we bought her from, sailed the boat alone on both shorter and longer trips for some years with approximately 40 nights spent onboard every

year, but as he was aging, he wanted to size up to a Bandhom 24 with almost standing headroom and admittedly a somewhat better liveaboard-standard.

We had a fresh westerly breeze gusting force 6 and charged out of Horsens Fjord past Vorsø, Alrø, Snaptun and Hjarnø to the small island Endelave in Kattegat, where we made landfall for the night in an almost empty harbour. We cooked a hot meal in the unheated sailors' quarter on shore with our alcohol heater under the table and enjoyed ourselves with a Netflix film on the iPad, before we hit the sack with sleeping bags under thick woolen blankets in minus 2^0 degrees keeping the hatch open. Next day the wind fell light to a force 3-4 and we eased close by Fynshoved a 100 metres from the beach and right under the nose of fisherman in waders with only a tiny and soft touchdown on the sandy bottom before reaching deeper water again in the Great Belt. You will find a film from this passage on Youtube.

Studies, moving to Copenhagen and competing activities eventually resulted in my being alone in charge of the boat with two boats to maintain and keep. I lent indefinitely to a young man, on condition that he maintains her and pays the insurance. He still sails her on the Bay of Køge.

17. FINDING MY WAY TO SEA

I have always been attracted by the magic of the sea. As a child my family moved to the Southern Jutland region, and I attended the independent school in Rødding headed by our teacher and headmaster Th. Hartvig Nielsen. He was as much a sailor and skipper, as he was our headmaster. So I was raised with a certain maritime decorum. It was called the bosun's principle. The older children were instructed in their leading role towards the younger ones in small groups (crews) when going on school camps and excursions.

We should take the first step and participate in anything, we were supposed to lead. Like digging a toilet, collecting firewood or caring for a campfire. Back then I never knew his first name, but he was known to all of us as Hartvig. A charismatic and temperamental gentleman with great love for us kids and a lionheart when going up against our parents, who had the greatest respect for him. We loved him as the children's friend and champion, he always was. He was a passionate man in anything he did, and it rubbed off on his teaching.

He built the first replica of a viking ship in Denmark in 1963 as a leader in the scout movement: Imme Gram as a replica of the Ladby ship found near Kerteminde. It was no coincidence, that our activities were dominated by the forest, nature and the vikings. Ranger skills and viking history were so much part of our school life, that we started building a viking ship based on the inspiration of Hartvig from Gotland image stones; Imme Slejpner, as she was named was was moored in the Genner Bay. The ship wasn't finished in our time at the school, and unfortunately I never got to sail it.

We built kayaks in canvas and GRP and sewed our own life jacket. It probably wouldn't have been accepted today, but our parents backed us and Hartvig. On a school trip with Hartvig's ship Håbet (Hope), an old water barge from Copenhagen, we reached Ærøskøbing from Aarøsund via Lyø, before the Ships Inspection grounded us and ordered us to go ashore. Only because we built our liferafts and made the life jackets on our own. There was not much sense of humour nor any pragmatic indulgence, but we stood 100% by Hartvig, who faced both public humiliation and a small shitstorm in the press. We had a strong community and a school for life in culture and formation.

Thus my yearning for sailing and the sea awakened.

The way I work, I went all-in on the interest and sought out books on the subject and places to learn the skills. My grand parents gave the book "I am a sailor" from Politiken Publishing house for my birthday, and I read it over and over again. Everything from navigation to anchoring, first aid at sea, as well as how to preserve eggs without having a cooling box onboard.

I took a navigation class in the youth night school in Jels in the middle of the country side one night a week for a year and got to know a chap with a Flipper dinghy. He taught me the basics of sailing on local lake of 1 nautical mile length, and we sailed back and forth for whole days of training.

I finished the navigation course with a proof of participation, which is the only formal navigational training I have. At 15 I lived together with my mother in Ribe in Southern Jutland after the divorce of my parents, where I began Optimist sailing and became junior instructor at the same time, I earned my A-sailor status, as I already had outgrown the Optimist. We sailed on the river close to the castle embankment and became rather experienced in sailing in strong currents. I took it all to heart and envisioned sailing far bigger waters.

My first command

I was totally obsessed with getting a ship of my own, dreamed about it at night and made drawings and fantasized about it during the day. Inbetween I did find time to tend to my studies in the gymnasium though.

My mother painting the hull of the rugged amateur built waterbike i. Ribe 1980.

Almost daily, I rode on my bicycle to Ribe Boatcenter, a local boatyard building the Diana 21, a GRP version of a classic slender motorboat of the 1930's often used for pleasure boating, hunting or fishing. Outside they often had a brokerage selection of rather odd boats, but I didn't see it that way. I only saw a ship under my command. Thus I became the proud owner of an amateur designed waterbike built in steel and glassfibre. My happiness lasted all the way through the refit, where it was sanded and painted. And right until

The moment of truth, when the vessel slides back into the water.

the celebratory speech at the launch with invited dignitaries and my mother, who was appointed voluntarily and had taken part in the paint job.

First mate Kristian and I were properly seamanly dressed and jumped onboard, when the contraption was heavily rested upon sliding back into its unsentimental wet element. Immediately the aft end of the vessel submerged and threatened to capsize backwards. Kristian made the wise decision of any rat, who knows what is good for it and abandoned ship for the safety of dry land. Being the responsible captain I stayed and counter balanced the vessel by leaning heavily forward.

In this way I was able to prove to my mum and the world press, that every thing was fine and dandy and even managed to sail some 20-30 metres - a bit like Howard Hughes in Spruce Goose - the world's largest water plane, that flew 1.6 km in 25 metres altitude once only in 1947.

A settlement was made with the boatyard regarding the unseaworthy excuse for a ship, and I swapped it for a retired diving dinghy with two catamaran hulls and a plywood deck between them. From water bike to a motorized launch. I was getting ahead of myself for sure. My father helped me with the last few kroner for buying an old 1.5 HP Seagull outboard built in 1969 and still going strong. I still have it in my possession. It is a two-stroke engine with 10% oil in the petrol and a starting chord, which is rolled around the top a few times and pulled very hard to start the engine with a tired roar. In this boat I embarked on numerous little expeditions on the river from Ribe to the lock protecting the flat land from the tidal mudflats.

The diving vessel "Mingo," in which I navigated the Ribe River with great patience when battling my way back against the current from the locks of the mudflats.

Below: My friend Poul seated on a camping chair and wearing one of our homemade life jackets embarked for a westbound expedition to the Kammerslusen locks.

18. INSPIRATIONAL SOURCES AND RECOMMENDED LITTERATURE

"Three Men i en Båd" by Jerome K. Jerome

"Tre Mand i en Sejlbåd" by Jan Ebert

"We didn't mean to go to sea" by Arthur Ransome

"The Dinghy Cruising Companion" by Roger Barnes

"Sailing Just for Fun - High adventure on a small budget" by A.C. Stock

Politikens "Jeg er sejler" by Bengt Kihlberg

"Riddle of the Sands" by Erskine Childers

"Mal sehen wie weit wir kommen" by Hans Habeck

"Lone across the seas" by Robin Lee Graham

"My Old Man and the Sea" by David Hays and Daniel Hays

"Up the Creek" by Tony James

"Wandering under Sail" by Eric Hiscock

"A History of Hurley Marine" by Tim Sharman and Nick Vass

"The Westerly Story" by Brian Eastal and Peter Poland

"Småbådssejads" by Åke Janheim

"Watercraft Magazine"

"Practical Boat Owner Magazine"

Websites:

da.wikipedia.org

hurleyownersassociation.co.uk

westerly-owners.co.uk

leisureowners.org.uk

visitfyn.dk/fyn/oplevelser/oehavsstien

Facebookgruppen "Dansk Pocket Yacht Club"

dansketursejlere.dk

Recognitions

I wish to thank my friend Uwe Gräfer, who leads the way in our friendship and contributed to the overview and clarity of this book project with intelligence and wit. And a special thanks if owed to his contribution with chapter 6 and his counsel on buying a 30-50 years old boat.

Many thanks to my wife Mette for lending an ear to my passion and for friendly participation and occasional interest in my boat talk and for countless cups of coffee and invigorating marshmallow mice on long passages in fresh or foul weather.

I would like to thank my sailing friend Jens Wellejus, my wife Mette and my sons Emil and Oscar for constructive criticism and proof reading. A special thanks is owed to John Machell for proof reading the English edition.

A special thanks I owe to photographer Peter Brøgger for the use of pictures of the Spækhugger Thor DEN 78 of KAS, covering the front page; The Spækhugger Pillen of Aarhus on page 145 and the depicted Albin Express also in this book.

I sincerely thank Nick Vass, Martin Sørensen, Bertram, André Christensen, Henrik Jæger, Ole Faurschou, Udo Nocera, Lars Lindholm, Gry Maria Kjaer Sørensen, Kristoffer Jensen, Søren Simonsen, Anders Lund, Lene Mi Ran and LM Windpower, Lars Ekelund, Leif Frank, Søren Simonsen, Søren Høyer, Claes Andersson, Håkan Wahrén and Norrköpings Segelsällskap, Bjarne Jensen, Henrik Ladegaard, Ulla Westermann, Flemming Palm, Knud Erik Schulz, Henrik Dinesen, Klaus Hinrichsen, Jørn Frøhlich, naval architect Gert Gerlach for allowing me access to Drabant documentation, Jim Quarnström, The Danish Seascouts, naval architect Lars Olsen for drawings of his design, the L23 and and that of his father Knud Olsen: Bandholm 24. Along with Peter Grönlund of Seacamper IF, Matt Newland and Lara Marsh of Swallow Yachts, Niels Tranekjer of International Yacht Sales, Sunbeam Yachts of Schöchl Yachtbau,

Pascal Ernst of Neptun Yachts as well as Frank Störck of Sailart for the many pictures of the mentioned boats.

I would also like to thank the different owners' associations, designers, boat yards and holders of copyrights for kindly making drawings and photographs available for the book. Through the wonderful effort put into the owners' associations, we are able to preserve the vast knowledge we have regarding the important sailing cultural heritage for posterity as well as the value these boats have to us. I would also encourage the readers to sign up for their respective associations and support the effort and engagement put into them.

Last but not least a great thanks to the "Dansk Pocket Yacht Club" group on facebook for enthusiasm and initial moral support and sparring enabling the creation of this book.

Rights to drawings and photographs

Where possible, I collected permissions from designers and boat yards, on other occasions from the clubs that organise the boats and preserve all the technical and historical documentation on the boats.

The Leisure Owners Association hold all rights to drawings and marketing material regarding Leisure yachts. You will find their website at: leisureowners.org.uk.

The Hurley Owners Association hold all rights to drawings and marketing material as well as original photographs from the early marketing of Hurley yachts. You will find their website at: hurleyownersassociation.co.uk. See also the facebook group "Hurley Owners Association. Hurley Yachts."

The L23 club is an active class association, maintaining a huge effort to keep racing activities going and arrange for trim weekends with focus on optimisation of the sailing as well as social gatherings. You will find their website at the address L23.dk.

LM-Owners Association collaborates with LM Windpower, who is the holder of rights with regard to LM-boats. You will find the LM club website here: lmklubben.dk.

The Folkboat owners association is doing a determined and targetted job of getting young people into sailing and aboard the Folkboats. Their website can be found at: folkebaad.dk.

Shrimper Owners Association Falmouth preserve the rights to photographs of the Cornish Shrimper 19. You will learn more about SOA on facebook.

All private photographs are made available by the credited owners, who preserve all rights to the pictures used in this book. All other pictures are the propoerty of the author.

No photographs or illustrations may be used without express permission by the author or the mentinoned rights holders, nor may they be printed, distributed or passed on in any digital or mechanical form.